The WISDOM
OF EMOTIONS

Happiness is a way of life !!

Dr. Dave

4-10-13

Building Genuine Happiness
and Finding Inner Peace

Dr. David F. Coppola

Foreword by Dr. Darren R. Weissman

CHOOSE LOVE
PRESS

Editorial supervision: Andrea Gollin
Jacket design: Xiao'nan Wang
Typesetting: Fusion Creative Works

Published by Choose Love Press
Hardcover ISBN: 978-0-9886888-0-3
Library of Congress Control Number: 2012955395

Publisher's Cataloging-in-Publication data
Coppola, David F.
    The wisdom of emotions : building genuine happiness and finding inner peace /
    Dr. David F. Coppola.
    p. cm.
    ISBN 978-0-9886888-0-3
1. Self-actualization (Psychology). 2. Mind and body. 3. Happiness. 4. Peace of mind.
5. Self-help techniques. I. Title.

BF637.S4 C665 2013
158 --dc23   2012955395

10987654321
1st edition, January 2013

For my wife, Susan

Submit to a daily practice.
Your loyalty to that
is a knock on the door.

Keep knocking, and the joy inside
will eventually open a window
and look out to see who's there.

— Rumi (1207-1273)

CONTENTS

FOREWORD

Lasting change and building genuine happiness begin with understanding that we live in an interactive reality whose architect is the mind. Then, to facilitate the shift your heart desires, you must make a conscious choice about how you'll live your life—the choice is between love and fear.

With such extremes, being able to interpret the wisdom of your emotions is fundamental to creating a genuinely happy life. Even further, to build genuine happiness and find inner peace, you have to probe beneath the surface to get to the root causes of fear, stress, chronic pain, disillusionment, or any other negatively perceived aspect of life. Creating sustainable change can be likened to the difference between reading about driving a car and actually getting behind the wheel. Experience is the greatest teacher.

My dear friend and colleague for the past twenty years, Dr. David Coppola, fondly known to his friends and patients as Dr. Dave, is offering you the power and the tools to choose love, a prism through which you can learn to see each and every experience, challenge or stressful situation—whether it's a health crisis, personal crisis or world crisis—as an opportunity to evolve and transform your life.

The heart of the matter of chronic pain, a broken heart, or not knowing how you'll pay your mortgage or put food on your table to feed your family has another purpose and meaning beyond the experience itself. This topic can be a very slippery slope; however, asking what I call the Truth Question helps to shape-shift the judgment you may be holding towards your body, relationships or life itself into a moment of conscious discernment. It is this single Truth Question that changes the entire game of life and thus compels you to take action and discover the wisdom of your emotions: "Given the opportunity, would you ever choose to create your life, a day, or even a single moment with any pain, fear or stress? Would you choose to be abused, have cancer, wake up depressed or anxious, lose your vision, or feel overwhelmed, angry, or fearful on any level?" The answer is obvious, and always: "Never!"

Knowing that no one ever consciously chooses any symptom, stress or disease, while at the same time everyone on the planet experiences them, leads us to ask: "Where do they come from?" Remember, the mind is the architect of life and everything in life is attracted via the emotional patterns broadcasting from the mind. Subconscious perceptual reality, or what is not a conscious thought, incubates in the recesses of our subconscious mind and forces us into a protective mode, thereby inhibiting our ability to attract something we want into our lives.

What may appear to be a negative experience of pain, fear or stress is actually what I refer to as The G.A.P. (The Gratitude Action Potential). The G.A.P. is a moment of subconscious protection that simultaneously graces us with the opportunity to learn, grow and change in a way that would otherwise never be known.

So many of the negative thought patterns we buy into about ourselves and others are actually subconscious emotions and core limiting beliefs stemming from environments we were raised in. These subconscious patterns create memories that when triggered cause the emotions and beliefs to rise to the surface of our conscious reality and take on a life of their own. The book you are holding is an action step and will equip you with practical tools, strategies, and understanding of the energy that's moving you—your emotions.

From my experience of developing The LifeLine Technique® (*See Appendix*), conducting well over one hundred thousand LifeLine sessions, and teaching people around the world the power within each of us to heal, regenerate and be whole, I have witnessed, many times, the sometimes mind-boggling and rapid transformation from fear to love, broken to whole, separateness to oneness. Get ready to transcend and transform walls of fear, judgment, and hatred. Get ready to discover the nature within you to embrace yourself and life with compassionate acceptance, forgiveness, gratitude and love.

In 1955, Reverend Martin Luther King, Jr. stated in Montgomery, Alabama, "Men often hate each other because they fear each other; they fear each other because they don't know each other; they don't know each other because they cannot communicate; they cannot communicate because they are separated." Has much changed in the past fifty-seven years? Have we learned from the hate, fear, misunderstanding, lack of communication and separation? Do *you* know the wisdom of *your* emotions?

Whether we're speaking about the relationships between cells, organs, glands, microorganisms, senses, or systems of the body or the personal and collective relationships of humanity, the wisdom of emotions is fundamental and essential for building genuine happiness.

FOREWORD

Fasten your seat belt and get ready to move at the speed of love. Dr. Coppola's knowledge and passionate way of teaching and writing distill quantum healing and conscious evolution into a practical philosophy for living.

Keep shining bright!

With Infinite Love & Gratitude,

Dr. Darren R. Weissman
Developer of The LifeLine Technique®

INTRODUCTION

Our true nature is to be happy. Happiness promotes an inner sense of peace and tranquility. It facilitates a knowing that everything is the way it should be. And happiness is not only an emotion, but a way of life. I believe happiness is at the top of everyone's list when it comes to emotions they want to experience. Although our choices regarding how we live are infinite, sometimes, the decisions we make can be distracting and may lead us astray—these are the choices that can make the state of happiness difficult to maintain.

Know that we have the power to choose; we can, with awareness and mindfulness, orchestrate a symphony of joy in our lives that will enhance our mental, physical and spiritual health. I have written this book to show you how to cultivate more wisdom and maintain happiness.

Despite the fact that we *want* to be happy, for many of us, happiness is not where we spend most of our time. The next time you go to the grocery store, the bank, the post office, look around. What percentage of the people you see seem happy to you? Chances are, not the majority. Many people, much of the time, are not happy—many of us experience happiness as an emotion that is elusive and fleeting. Instead, we are all too familiar with negative emotions such as anxiety, worry, sadness, frustration or anger. In fact, some of us find it very easy to get to those negative places. Once we are there, experiencing an emotion such as anger, it can be difficult to shift our mood—we may not even realize that we *can* shift our mood.

We don't consciously succumb to negative feelings; we don't deliberately choose, for example, to feel helpless or hopeless. But prolonged negative states of being do happen and for some people they even become habitual. I'm here to tell you that life doesn't have to be this way and that it *should not* be this way.

Happiness and other positive emotions—including gratitude, hope, enthusiasm, peace and love—are our birthright. Our purpose is to thrive, not to live in negativity and not to merely survive. A positive emotional state is attainable for everyone. Some of us have simply gotten out of the habit.

Why am I telling you these things about happiness and your emotions? Why does happiness matter? In addition to feeling better emotionally, cultivating positivity has a major impact on our physical health. The reverse is true as well—negative emotions can have a negative effect on our health.

One of the key tools I use to build genuine happiness in my own life and those of my patients is through learning and living the principles of The LifeLine Technique®, which I explain in greater depth in the Appendix. As a result of learning this invaluable method, I am able to facilitate the healing of any health concern with greater effectiveness and efficiency than with any other modality I know of. The method also provides the framework for me to make important decisions with clarity. The LifeLine Technique empowers its users to embrace change, which is the essence of life, and helps us to get back to living on purpose. But the technique is simply a tool—you don't *need* The LifeLine Technique to achieve healing. Anyone can cultivate positivity and anyone can activate healing in his/her life.

I wrote *The Wisdom of Emotions* to help you effectively process your emotions and more easily access positive feelings. When you learn to maintain a positive emotional state, you are able to live life to the fullest in all arenas—from your relationships to your career to your physical, mental and spiritual health.

I have spent the past eighteen years as a chiropractic physician, practicing holistic medicine and acupuncture. During that time I have successfully treated thousands of people for all kinds of health issues. For the first five years of my career, my practice was what you would consider a traditional chiropractic approach. I provided relief for people suffering from headaches, neck pain and low back pain. But about thirteen years ago, my approach to my patients' health went through a radical transformation when I came to understand that unresolved emotional issues were underlying and contributing to physical complaints.

Once I began working with my patients to investigate the emotional issues at stake, bring awareness to those issues, and resolve them, my practice underwent a sea change. My patients' lives were transformed, as was my own. Patients didn't merely resolve physical complaints such as sore backs, necks and shoulders much faster and more effectively than before, but they began to fashion richer, more rewarding lives for themselves.

I have spent years studying holistic approaches. I have traveled the world to learn Traditional Chinese Medicine and Indian Ayurvedic Medicine with doctors including Deepak Chopra and Vasant Lad. I have deepened my understanding

4

of health *care* by incorporating traditional Eastern methods with my knowledge of Western approaches such as chiropractic, physiotherapy and The LifeLine Technique. All of my studying has been in the service of one goal—to increase my body of knowledge and the techniques at my disposal so I can more effectively teach and coach my patients and help them achieve optimal health.

When I talk about shifting your orientation to live in a more positive emotional state, I am not saying that your life will be free of challenges, or that you will walk around in a perpetual state of bliss. That would not be authentic, but neither is living with constant anxiety or anger. Nor am I saying that this emotional shift happens instantaneously. It takes time, attention and resolve to change. It takes learning to recognize and appreciate that everyday challenges are opportunities, chances to learn, grow and be creative. The ultimate goal of this practice? To achieve and maintain a state of inner tranquility and emotional stability. When our base state is peaceful and stable, we can respond more effectively and efficiently to life's many challenges.

How do we make this shift? Emotions were designed by our Creator to be our inner guidance system. When we are not sufficiently aware of our emotions, or we deny or disconnect from those emotions, our ego runs rampant and problems arise.

Remember when you were a child. Shy, embarrassing, angry and shameful moments seemed to linger only briefly before resolving and then, magically soon were forgotten. One difference between childhood and adulthood is the lingering process of emotions. As adults we tend to wallow in toxic emotions, making it more difficult to find a way back to the desired states of peace and happiness. As children this transitional state is fairly short. As adults it can linger for days, weeks, months and even years. It's because adults have well-developed egos.

Egotistic actions in adults feed combativeness and the need for revenge. These thoughts and actions severely damage our innate potential to forgive and show compassion. Thus, when we are counseled to be more child-like—as Deepak Chopra taught me—this is a truly valuable lesson.

When emotions are acknowledged and expressed appropriately and when we have support mechanisms, we can maintain moral order by choosing to practice loving-kindness and boundless compassion.

In these pages, I will discuss how honestly "feeling" your emotions contributes to your ability to be more positive. I will teach you how to be more aware of your support mechanisms. The more you learn to acknowledge and process your emotions, the more truthful your life will become, and the easier it will be to act mindfully.

INTRODUCTION

The knowledge in these pages is intended to enhance your ability to learn and grow to become a better *you*, not better than anyone else, not a *different* you, but *more* you—more truthful, more authentic. In short, who you are meant to be.

As a health care provider, nothing makes me happier than seeing my patients thrive. But I am limited in the amount of patients I can directly serve. That's why I'm writing this book—to share with a larger audience what I have learned through decades of study and practice.

Confucius says, "There is no one who does not eat or drink. But there are few who really know flavor." This book teaches you how to truly taste life, be it bitter or sweet. It teaches you how to feel your emotions (both negative and positive), how to gain wisdom from these emotions, and how, in turn, to live a more authentic life.

Chapter One

THE UNIVERSAL HEALING FREQUENCY

Infinite love & gratitude.

— Dr. Darren R. Weissman

Linda is a fifty-five-year-young woman who practices yoga and meditates every morning. She eats very healthy foods, despite peanut butter and chocolate cravings at night, and she moves through the world in a carefree, joyful state most of the time. She smiles and laughs daily and deals with stressors effectively. However, Linda was not always like this. Life, as she puts it, has not always been peaches and cream. Unfortunately, she was emotionally and sexually abused when she was younger, which led to a good deal of suffering. For many years, she wallowed in anger and resentment, regularly experienced serious road rage, and blamed the early mistreatment for her problems.

She came to see me when she decided to take responsibility for her life and change the course she was on. She realized that blaming her past was no longer serving her well. She truly wanted to change the way she perceived life.

While Linda had made an enormous amount of progress on her own, much of it on an intellectual level, she needed help to get her out of her terrible funk. That's when I met her. Our meeting was proof of the saying, "When the student is ready, the teacher will appear."

Together, we embarked on a journey of healing that involved learning, among other things, that thoughts are things. Thoughts are measurable frequencies that run through our bodies and affect the way we feel. More importantly, I taught Linda, as I will teach you, to be consistent in maintaining a healing frequency. The healing frequency I taught her is achieved by repeatedly thinking and/or saying the mantra "infinite love & gratitude."

After six months of working together, all was going as Linda had hoped and I had predicted. Linda was progressing well. She was learning to be more aware of her emotional state and to process negative emotions rather than get stuck in them. As a result, she was becoming more resilient and more positive. We were working on developing patience and finding forgiveness. It was at that point in Linda's treatment that a life-threatening experience became the ultimate teacher.

I was driving home to the Florida Keys from my Coral Gables office, prepared to enjoy a well-deserved break from what I like to call a day of healing the world. I was thinking about my plans to play tennis with my wife and wondering what to prepare for dinner when I got a call from my office manager. Linda had called my office in a crisis. She was having chest pain and was feeling delirious. She was having a heart attack. My office manager had her call 911 right away and she was rushed by ambulance to the hospital.

I reversed course in a New York minute and headed for Mariners Hospital in Tavernier, Florida. My immediate thoughts? I was scared and angry. There was no way I was going to let someone die who was so dedicated to cultivating positivity and who was on the verge of emotional freedom.

When I arrived at the emergency room, the tests confirmed a myocardial infarction. The physician said she was probably going to need open heart surgery and they were not equipped to do it there. Linda was being prepared to be airlifted in fifteen minutes to Jackson Memorial Hospital in Miami. Linda requested that I perform a healing on her. I knew that if I was able to work with her, it could have an enormous impact. Thankfully, I was granted permission to treat her. I had fifteen minutes.

I believe that the human body is self-healing when it is balanced emotionally, physiologically and structurally, while vibrating with the power of infinite love & gratitude. In my opinion, this is not a profound or esoteric statement—it is knowledge we all intuitively know, but that many of us bury in our busy, modern-day lives. For me, learning The Lifeline Technique® *(see Appendix)* brought this knowledge to my conscious awareness and has helped me facilitate healing for thousands of patients. I knew that Linda's heart attack was caused by her heart crying out for more joy and love—the heart is fed by joy. Linda was flat on her back on a cot with a tube in her nose, attached to an IV and hooked up to a series of monitors, but even in the middle of all of that, she seemed peaceful. When she saw me, her eyes lit up. In the months of being my patient, Linda had experienced a good deal of transformation and through her personal evolution, she had come to share my beliefs about healing. Was there a shadow of doubt in her? In me? Maybe…an emergency room and a life-threatening situation is not exactly an oasis of calm and quiet in which to summon up thoughts of infinite love & gratitude. Despite the circumstances, I wasn't willing to give up hope for a miraculous recovery. Neither was she.

I began by softly reassuring Linda that she was pure love. I looked into her eyes and told her we both needed to envision the arteries to her heart as open and flowing with light and love. As love flows in and around your heart, I said, the blood will nourish the muscle tissue and instantly promote healing. She looked into my eyes with hope and belief. I instructed her to close her eyes and imagine herself surrounded by white light and to "feel" joy in knowing she was in good and extremely competent hands. "We have the best emergency medicine in the world here," I said to soothe her. I continued to work with Linda, using The Lifeline Technique to identify the subconscious patterns affecting her heart health and harmonize them.

I was able to complete the treatment before Linda was airlifted to Miami. When she got to Jackson Memorial Hospital a complete cardiac work-up found no damage to her heart. The doctors couldn't explain what had happened but they were happy to send her home a few days later after inserting a stent in a partially occluded coronary artery for preventative care.

To this day, Linda jokes about the helicopter ride and the aftermath. In many ways, treating Linda under such pressure, with minimal time during life-threatening circumstances, was the ultimate challenge for me as a doctor. She made my job easier though, because she was willing to join with me to do the hard work of harnessing her beliefs and intentions for healing. And we did it, we succeeded. We created our reality and manifested spontaneous healing. It was all about belief, intention and vibrating on the universal healing frequency of *love*.

These days, nearly a year after her heart attack, Linda is feeling great. She continues to see me for wellness care and life coaching. She maintains a positive attitude and no longer is trapped in the negative legacy of her past. She truly believes she is worthy and deserves to be happy. Anyone who has ever had to deal with issues similar to Linda's knows how profound the shift is to transition from feeling like a victim to feeling worthy and happy. She transformed her life by taking responsibility for it, by realizing that we all manifest our own reality.

MANIFESTING REALITY

"We manifest our own reality"—that is a phrase we hear a lot. But what does manifesting our reality actually mean? Simply put, it is the process by which our *thoughts* become our *experiences*. In other words, we see what we expect to see, what we are looking to see. If we believe that life is difficult and that people are mean, we will see difficulties and meanness. If we believe that life presents us with gifts on a daily basis and that people are noble, we will look every day for gifts (and find them), and we will see nobility.

We become aware of our reality through our senses—by seeing, hearing, smelling, tasting and feeling. Our brains process information that is transmitted through electrical impulses and the protein receptors in our eyes, ears, nose, mouth and skin because that is *how* we perceive our world.

What does manifesting entail? Haven't you ever heard someone say something like, "Give me something I can actually hold in my hand? Show me something that I can see with my own eyes. *Then* I'll believe." These statements come from people who have a hard time with abstract thinking and metaphysics. Dr. Wayne Dyer, a great spiritual leader and teacher of Taoism, wrote a book titled *You'll See It When You Believe It*. It wasn't titled *I'll Believe It When I See It*, as we have been conditioned to say. The latter saying is a telling example of how thought viruses make it difficult to develop wisdom and how they delay spiritual maturity for many in our culture until the age of seventy or eighty.

But recently we are seeing a positive shift—people in their thirties and forties are realizing that yes, we *do* manifest our reality, and as a consequence many younger folks are diving into spiritual practice and becoming more emotionally stable. As a whole, we are becoming wiser at a much younger age and finding ways to build a new world; a world filled with joy, created from positivity.

To know that we manifest our reality takes awareness and discipline. It takes being fearless. FEAR, when it is not based on a life or death situation, is basically *Forgetting Everything's All Right*. To consciously and habitually work to create the life we want to live, we need to put more time into abstract thinking and allow that to be a major contributor to learning and growing. So, how do we start to manifest our reality? Two keys are: (1) allow ourselves to believe in the power of the mind, and (2) do our best to truly understand the Law of Attraction.

BELIEVING IS KNOWING

When it comes to manifesting our reality, there are differences between *knowing, believing* and *imagining*. But the human mind does not recognize these differences. The human mind will respond as it has been programmed. I have long been intrigued by a quote from personal-success author Napoleon Hill, "What the mind of man can conceive and believe, it can achieve." Can you imagine world peace being perpetuated by practices of inner peace? Peace is a vision for many people and will manifest as more and more of us begin to *know* and *believe* in the process of world peace through inner peace.

The hundredth monkey effect is documented scientific research that involved monkeys inhabiting two separate Japanese islands. A group of monkeys started washing their food before eating. Apparently washing it made the food taste better and provided greater nourishment. Well, once the hundredth monkey participated in this new ritual of washing food before eating, there was a miraculous co-existent ritual started by monkeys on an adjacent island. This breakthrough evidence has shown us that if new behaviors are practiced and synchronized among enough people, a critical mass of energy can be reached, thereby allowing new behaviors to spread. We *will* live to see the day when we all live in a more beautiful and peaceful world. But first, you gotta believe.

Have you ever heard of a vision board? It is one tool to help you achieve your goals—to manifest your reality in a positive way. You cut out pictures and/or words related to your hopes and dreams and paste them on a poster board that you hang in your home, in a spot where you will see it and read it every day and be reminded of these positive goals. The actions of seeing and reading create electromagnetic frequencies (EMF). These EMFs radiate off and out of your brain and, by properties explained in quantum physics, come together to manifest your desires. The EMFs are aligning with your physical world, thereby attracting things, people and events that create what you envisioned or wished for. I am not going to overwhelm you with the science, but these are the basic principles of the Law of Attraction. You will become better at creating your reality as you practice what is taught in this book. But please realize that manifesting reality takes more than just thinking and envisioning. It takes acting and believing.

Another example of how reality is manifested is evident in the actual combination of the two theories explained above—the hundredth monkey effect and the Law of Attraction. I believe these theories can explain why the Boston Red Sox finally won the World Series in 2004. The team had the talent, coaching staff, and ability to win many times before the 2004 team put it all together. In fact, the team made it to the World Series several times since winning it in 1918. It just took eradicating the bambino curse and a little more belief by the massive fan base. So get ready, Chicago fans. The Cubs, who haven't won a World Series since 1908, will probably be the next team to overcome their championship drought! They just need to transform their widely accepted designation of "the lovable losers."

THE BAMBINO CURSE

On October 23, 2004, the Boston Red Sox finally won the World Series, thereby abolishing the "bambino curse" after eighty-six years. This curse had become a self-fulfilling prophecy—we believed in it and it unfortunately manifested in heart-breaking losses several times when the Red Sox were on the brink of winning.

The bambino curse was the legacy of a deal the Red Sox made in 1919 when they sold baseball star George Herman ("Babe") Ruth, Jr., a.k.a. the "bambino," for $125,000 to their dreaded rivals, the New York Yankees.

The bambino curse was the "belief" that selling their star player put a hex on the team that led to over eight decades of never winning the World Series—years of mental and emotional anguish for Boston sports fans around the world!

Boston fans suffered from the belief that we were cursed—until the tide changed. As the team was about to win the World Series in 2004 our beliefs changed—we believed that the curse was broken! When it came to Game 4, already having won the first three games, the Red Sox never trailed and completed the sweep of the St. Louis Cardinals. We now *know* we can win it all, again and again, and proved this in 2007. It will be a long time though, until we catch up to the class act in pinstripes 'cause they've got a lot of championships under their belt. But, Red Sox fans, you gotta *believe*!

Knowing is believing! And believing is another key to manifesting reality.

WHAT ARE EMOTIONS?

Here is a very important scientific fact: *thoughts are a measurable form of energy*. All of our episodic mind-centered activity creates a flow of energy. This energy flows throughout our bodies. And this energy can actually be measured and categorized.

If I were to put electrodes on my forehead and around my heart and think about something that gets me angry, like the Yankees beating the Red Sox, I will get a frequency response on an oscilloscope, which is a measuring device for revealing electromagnetic frequencies.

If I were to think of a roller coaster ride, the oscilloscope would reveal a different frequency or response to the thought of excitement. If I had relaxing thoughts of sitting on a beach in the Bahamas, sipping an exotic drink with an umbrella in it while looking out over the soft, white, sandy beaches and green ocean, I would still get another different frequency response on the oscilloscope. What these frequency responses are measuring is actually *vibrations* that run through the body as they are transformed into what we call *emotions*.

The interesting thing is that the electromagnetic frequencies associated with thoughts pertaining to anger, excitement or tranquility are similar in everybody. However, differences become apparent when it comes to the *expression* of the emotion. Take anger, for example. Some people yell or scream, some remain tight-lipped, some people throw things or lash out with vengeance, and others retreat from the scene and enter into their own world, fed by other negative experiences.

Given these vastly different ways of expressing the same emotion, it becomes very clear that people are individuals. Reactions to the same emotion vary from person to person. Realizing that these variations in responses exist helps us to understand each other better.

Emotion, in English, is a perfect word for what it represents: "E-motion," or "energy" in motion. This explanation helps us understand what emotions really are: *frequencies and vibrations that travel through the body*. And as they travel through the body, emotions trigger various biochemical and structural responses that elicit what is better known as feelings. When toxic, these feelings are the underlying cause of imbalances that create health problems and related symptoms.

Brilliant and unprecedented scientific research by Candace Pert, Ph.D., is presented in her book, *Molecules of Emotion*. Her research proves to us that we actually have molecules, or "specialized cells," that reflect emotion. These cells are found in all organs, glands, systems and regions of the human body.

The emotions we "sense" travel up and down tracks or channels in our bodies, which Traditional Chinese Medicine (TCM) calls "meridians." Both the meridians and our emotions are not physical by nature. However, our emotions run through our bodies, just like electrical impulses are transmitted throughout our nervous systems, and blood runs through our arteries and veins.

The Chinese have taught us to recognize these energies running through our body as "qi" (pronounced "chee"). The people of India call this energy "prana" and Christians around the world call this energy "holy spirit." In essence it is "love", expressing itself the best way it can under the circumstances.

We call our emotions "feelings" because we harbor them in our bodies. In working with patients, I have found that when someone internalizes, or holds in the body, a toxic feeling like anger, it leads to overall fatigue and then, over time, can lead to physical problems and even illness.

A TOXIC EMOTION: ANGER

You may have wondered why people who hold onto anger are not only easily irritated but are often tired and may have multiple health complaints. The reason for this is because anger is a frequency that affects the liver, according to thousands of years of accumulated knowledge imparted to us from Traditional Chinese Medicine.

My patient Jim's experience can help us better understand the role of emotions in illness and health care. Jim is a fifty-five-year-young triathlete. When I started treating him, he had been on the cholesterol-lowering statin drug Lipitor for a few years. Based on his lifestyle, you would think Jim's cholesterol levels would be within normal range due to his regular cardiovascular exercise and his balanced approach to nutrition, but instead it was through the roof at 298 (the normal range is 150-180 according to Western medicine). His ratio of good-to-bad cholesterol though, was not far off what is considered normal. What I quickly realized from examining Jim was that despite his high level of physical conditioning, his liver was not functioning optimally. Elevated cholesterol levels can result from the body's unresolved response to anger. This was the case with Jim—his liver was not functioning optimally due to his internalization of anger, which is a toxic emotion. When Jim got angry he would get red in the face and become completely silent. He buried the anger deep in his liver.

Jim's goal was to get off of Lipitor and to lower his cholesterol using natural remedies. I started treatment by introducing a cleanlier metabolized supplement called red yeast rice to gently stimulate proper cholesterol levels for Jim. Red yeast rice is an herb used in alternative medicine that mimics the pharmacokinetics of statin drugs. The pharmaco-dynamics of red yeast rice minimize the interference at the neuromuscular junction caused by using statin drugs. For Jim, this meant that his recovery time after training shortened once he was off Lipitor. Additionally, his soreness from his intense workouts was minimized by adding massage and chiropractic care to his weekly treatment protocol.

However, the underlying cause of imbalance to Jim's liver function remained—his conditioned response of internalizing his anger and being tight-lipped in difficult situations. Jim was completely unaware of this dynamic—he had no consciousness of his own anger or of his responses to it. His outward appearance was one of great calm, although his fingernails were bitten to the quick. This was an example of a negative emotion producing a subconscious protective reaction.

Working with Jim to help him become aware of his habitual response to anger and the effects it was having on his body was a crucial step. It only took a couple of visits for this realization to become important enough for Jim to change. I used The LifeLine Technique to harmonize his thoughts and expressive tendencies to the universal healing frequency of "infinite love & gratitude." Using a holistic approach provided Jim with the awareness he needed to match his patterns of behavior to his symptoms. I provided him the tools needed to recognize when he was experiencing anger along with guidance to follow the steps necessary to reach his goal.

He allowed himself to respect his feelings, express anger constructively, and let it go. It took about six months of working together for this shift to manifest—considering that his responses were deeply ingrained over a lifetime, this was impressive progress. While his goal was to lower his cholesterol, which he achieved, by nearly one hundred points, an added benefit was an overall improvement in his fitness level and racing times. In fact, he has won several first place awards in his age bracket at international triathlons in the past couple of years.

What if it were you in Jim's position, and you did not have easy access to someone like me who could work with you to harmonize your thoughts and expressive tendencies using this technique? Can you still effect the changes in your life that Jim has in his? Absolutely. Awareness and intent are the keys to making these important changes. The Lifeline Technique, while a valuable tool, is not a magic bullet. You, however, are—you hold all of the power to make these changes through awareness. Whether you work with a therapist, a life coach, or on your own, you can learn to observe how you process negative emotions, where you get stuck, what you don't express, how your body feels, and through careful attention and resolve, you can transform your life.

Once you put this knowledge into practice you will begin to witness many positive changes in your life. You will be living life with increased integrity and that in turn will result in more energy and positivity. The more attuned you are to your emotions and past negative patterns, the more you allow yourself to experience and then let the feelings go, the better your will feel.

A TOXIC EMOTION: WORRY

Like anger, worry is an all-too-common toxic emotion. Can you recall times when you were nervous about a public speech or a challenging encounter and felt sick to your stomach? That is worry. Physically, our *stomach* tends to speak to us with symptoms when we experience worry and anxiety; these feelings can be the underlying cause of stomach-related distress including ulcers, indigestion and heartburn.

Sarah is a forty-year-young woman who suffers from esophageal reflux disease and abdominal bloating, commonly known as heartburn and indigestion. When Sarah became my patient, she had been popping antacids for about eight years. She started taking antacids at the recommendation of her obstetrician, who suggested she take them for temporary relief when she was pregnant. That was a mistake from the start! Antacids alter the normal pH of the stomach, making it more alkaline for transient relief. After taking antacids, the stomach pH rises and consequently the body is forced to produce hydrochloric acid to restore the proper pH for digestion. Do you see where this is heading? Continued exposure to antacids leads to continued flushing of acid. This perpetuates overly acidic environs, not only providing an environment for flourishing *H.pylori* bacteria, the cells responsible for duodenal ulcers, but for cancerous growths in the gastrointestinal tract.

In my opinion, Sarah's symptoms were a result of worry and anxiety she experienced as a first-time mom-to-be, and her obstetrician was not completely on target in how he addressed her issues. She was only three months pregnant when he recommended antacids, so crowding and crushing of the stomach was not the issue. Western medicine often helps many people, but with conditions such as Sarah's, there are other more effective and natural ways to treat heartburn and indigestion. Why aim to overpower and hammer down symptoms when there are gentler and more holistic approaches?

What does it mean to treat someone holistically? Holistic practitioners assess your whole self: your emotional, nutritional, biochemical, structural and spiritual needs, rather than simply investigating where a symptom is most apparent. Holistic practitioners then "treat" by administering the most effective, natural and appropriate procedures and approaches for the detected imbalances, which will in turn support your body to achieve the balance it takes to heal naturally. Holistic healing is not intended to serve as a band-aid or a one-time fix, although people often experience immediate relief. Instead, holistic healing is an ongoing journey to ultimately living a healthier, more conscious and better life.

When I coach patients who are on multiple and/or inappropriate drugs back to health, I tell them to be thankful for the medicine(s) they are using, but that they now have awareness of gentler and more holistic approaches. When we can substitute natural remedies for prescription or over-the-counter medications, it helps minimize the biochemical invasion and imbalances pharmaceutical drugs cause, otherwise known as side effects. I have my patients repeat after me, depending on the drug, as follows: "Thank you Prevecid (or Nexium, or Tagamet, or Prilosec, etc.), but I don't need you anymore! Thank you for helping me, but now I choose to be more natural in my approach to overcoming these symptoms of heartburn and indigestion."

I do not want to bash Western medicine, which is actually quite miraculous with its emergency protocol. However, problems can arise because medical doctors today are trained to treat symptoms and do not always identify the cause of disease or illness. To further complicate matters, in my opinion, many medical doctors are overly influenced by the powerful pharmaceutical companies. Some brilliant medical professionals like Andrew Weil and Deepak Chopra have blended Western medicine with more holistic philosophies to greatly benefit their patients. I extend a sincere thank you to these doctors and the many more who are realizing the efficacy of a holistic approach to health care. The holistic approach looks at the entire person and goes beyond the symptoms to investigate and treat the root cause of distress.

In the above example we must respect the fact that Sarah was raised like many Americans, taking a pill whenever the slightest illness arose. Granted, people want a quick and easy fix, but usually a pill is only a band-aid, not a cure. After some truly amazing advances of Western medicine such as developing vaccines and virtually eradicating diseases like polio, it is understandable that so many Americans, like Sarah, accept and believe in Western medicine.

To help Sarah, I started gently by introducing a full spectrum enzyme formula for better digestion proficiency, as enzymes act like catalysts to make things happen in the body. I then addressed the cause of her digestive issues: the way she processed worry, and even deeper beneath that, the core issue, which was that she didn't know how to love herself. Sarah had a tendency to worry about the future and prepare for the worst. This is a common practice for people who live in a cause-and-effect world. I worked with Sarah and harmonized the detrimental "worst case scenario" thought patterns to the universal healing frequency of "infinite love & gratitude" and coached her on how to prepare for the *best*. After just three treatments geared to harmonizing the negative thought patterns, she was able to focus on positive thinking and prepare for the best to happen so she could truly and fully enjoy it. After all, most of the time good things happen when you use the power of positive thinking, so why not prepare to enjoy life instead of bracing against imaginary future disaster?

I taught Sarah to practice mini-meditations to help her deal with stress. To further improve her digestion, I taught her to maintain a proper food plan that included drinking more pure, filtered water with a little lemon (which helps to naturally alkalize the body). Chiropractic adjustments have helped her develop better posture and alleviate pain between the shoulder blades, which can contribute to nerve interference to the stomach region. It was important to teach her to appreciate and love herself so that she would treat herself well and truly practice being kind to herself, a thought that, curiously, is foreign to many people. Yet we cannot be truly kind to others unless we are first able to be kind to ourselves. One cannot give from empty pockets.

These practices are learned behaviors that start deliberately and gradually become second nature. They are not changes that happen in an afternoon, but over the course of time, with attention and commitment.

Chapter Two

THE KEY TO HAPPINESS

*The anticipation of something good happening in
one's life is the greatest joy.*
— Frank Hawkins

My friend Frank Hawkins, an entrepreneur and author, once expressed the above truth. I not only agree, but also would like to consider the reverse—our reactions when something bad happens. If merely thinking about something good that hasn't happened yet is our greatest joy, then how do we respond to the reality of something bad that has actually happened? Would something bad then become our greatest misery? I would say not only is that not the case, but that life's misfortunes are often our greatest teachers. How we react to unfortunate events is a major determining factor in the quality of our lives.

FIND THE "GOOD" IN EVERYTHING

Remember the adage, "Everything happens for a reason?" Well, it's true! And I would add a postscript to that—not only does everything happen for a reason, but there is likely good to be found in that reason. Think about these other popular sayings: "It is in these trying times that the cream rises to the top," and "After a storm, the trees still standing have stronger roots and their bark grows a little thicker." These sayings all relate to the same basic principle, that of finding the good in the midst of difficulty. Here, I present some strategies on how to find the good. It is up to you, however, to put these practices into action in your own life.

When you make the commitment to look for goodness, the doors open to the wondrous possibility of transforming negative to positive. It is in this shift—which is *not* the same as ignoring the negative—that you will find the basis for developing healthy habits to stabilize yourself emotionally, even during trying times, so you can see the other side of the coin and access the infinite possibilities available to you in life.

You may be thinking: "How do you do it?" Quite simply, you begin. Start tomorrow morning by waking up with a smile on your face. This can be accomplished by beginning your day with happy thoughts. Everyone can imagine something happy. It doesn't have to be the happiest thing in the world, just something leading you to inner peace and joy. Do not start your day by stressing out about all the work you've got to do, or by telling yourself you will never catch up with all your work. Instead, start with positive statements. Be happy you have a cup of coffee or spot of tea waiting for you. Be happy you have a fresh croissant or a bowl of cereal to eat. Do I need to remind you that there are people who don't even have a piece of bread in their cupboard? Thank God for another day to live, love and laugh. If you think that's too religious, thank the sun for rising and giving you light and warmth in which to live.

Daily tasks, even those that may seem challenging or overwhelming, will get done as you become more organized and plan to take on one task at a time. The first thing in the morning is not the time for blame, worry or complaints. Nor is morning the time for questioning your ability to be happy. Above all, do not wake up and begin cataloging your grudges from the day before—that will only lead to beginning the new day angry or acting mean. This approach—of holding so tight to grievances—will drain you and can lead to depression. Instead, smile. Just do it. Even if you don't feel like it, you can fake it. Smiling is a great habit. The sooner you can maintain a smile on your face, the sooner you will consistently feel better.

When I say find the good in everything, there are certain circumstances where the good is readily apparent. It's easy to see the good in your team winning the national championship. The whole city gets more recognition and thrives on the excitement. Restaurants are packed while stores and street vendors prosper from the sale of sports memorabilia. It's not difficult to see the good in a year of perfect weather for grapes to flourish in wine country and farmers to reap high crop production. It's hard to deny the benefits and the goodness in the philanthropic nature of the American Red Cross and the United Way.

But where is the good in the demolition resulting from hurricanes and other natural disasters such as tornados and earthquakes? What good can possibly be found in the tragedies stemming from acts of terrorism? These disasters can usher in extremely trying times. But enduring trying times may help you grasp the true meaning of life and appreciate what the important things in life really are. You can overcome these challenges—you can overcome *any* challenge—as long as you realize the truth, which is that you are more powerful than you know. We must realize that the universe would not present challenges to us unless we can handle them. If adversity seems to leave you feeling debilitated, stop doubting your outstanding ability to rise to the occasion. Remember, the cream *always* rises to the top.

FROM ADVERSITY COMES STRENGTH

How do you react when something bad happens? Do you learn anything from the experience? Can you find the good in it? Can anything positive come from a car accident? Can any good result from failing a class in school or losing a job? What can possibly be good about losing a house to a bank foreclosure? These are all serious challenges that people face. Many people, when presented with these kinds of situations, will not respond by looking for the good, and will not consider that the cloud may have a silver lining. Instead, some people will blame the world for not providing them with a paradise of joy to inhabit. Then there are those, feeling envious, who will look around and compare themselves with others, questioning why someone else is so lucky. They might ask: "Why was *he* given the gift of multi-millionaire parents?"

Some people blame God for seemingly not being there when they needed Him. "How can God let this happen?" they ask. Others will ruminate on their negative experiences and refuse to let go, saying things such as: "Why has this happened to me? I really cannot forgive this." Some will wallow in the injustices of their childhood and blame certain circumstances, including illness and disease, or past events, or a friend or relative who has taken advantage of them. "Oh, woe is me…"

Perhaps you have experienced some of the unfortunate events listed above or other similar events. After all, these are real life occurrences, and they are not uncommon. It's unfortunate if you have been faced with difficulties in the past, but you must not allow such misfortunes to dictate your life in the present or shape your future. In order to regain happiness and health, get back on track to creating an enriching, joyful life for yourself. Make a profound *shift* in the way you process difficult life experiences. Now is the time to start! You have picked up this book for a reason. Within these pages are the tools and strategies to make positive change happen, to get going, to move forward and truly live your life.

Does my reaction to negative events sound uncaring or dismissive or even cold to you? Does it make you want to say: "Yes, but what happened to me is so much worse…" If so, you may be clinging to a negative experience, which in turn can lead to cultivating trouble, and/or feeling stuck. Ask yourself: Am I someone who practices blaming others for shortcomings and negative experiences in life? If so, recognize and realize that you are doing this, and stop. If not, you probably know people who do this and if so, you should get them a copy of this book and be a support mechanism for them. They need you!

Maybe you have not been able to forgive someone or something for "causing" your particular ordeals. Forgive others, forgive the world, and, most importantly, forgive yourself. Now is the time, now is *your* time. Start gathering your tools, strategies and support systems and make the commitment to positive change. It is not always easy to change, but change is the essence of life and is essential to your growth and well-being.

Forgiveness is an area where many of us can use a lot of work—it is critically important, yet many of us are not very good at forgiveness and are unfortunately not in the habit of forgiving. Yet, forgiving is one of the most important tools in terms of creating a fulfilled life. The realm of forgiveness is a sanctuary for knowing love. First, we need to forgive ourselves for all the times we couldn't overcome challenges.

The healing vibration begins with your choice to forgive. Start making healthier choices. With every choice there is a consequence, and it doesn't have to be a bad one. There is something to learn from every experience, although to do so it helps to remain aware of your support systems, your healing strategies and your vast capacity to change. Moving on from the "bad things" that have happened to you is imperative. Do your best to not rationalize and blame. Forgive, accept and release toxic energy by practicing the techniques presented in this book. Remember, happiness is a way of life. Start now by learning and practicing the principles of the Opponent Process Theory.

THE OPPONENT PROCESS THEORY

We often find ourselves living busy, hectic lives in which we feel trapped in the mode of "putting out fires," so to speak, and we get caught up in a "cause-and-effect" lifestyle. Instead of creating our reality, we are too busy reacting to problems arising from seemingly uncontrollable instances. One of the ways I teach my patients to get back to (or get to) creating their reality is by practicing the principles of the opponent process theory, which requires awareness and willingness to positively influence the flow of emotions. The opponent process theory teaches us to change the way we look at things. As Dr. Wayne Dyer says, "When we change the way we look at things, the things we look at change." According to the opponent process theory, the positive side of polar opposites—such as anger to joy, anxiety to calm, or fear to hope—is more easily attainable when living in present-time consciousness.

We must first recognize and appreciate that achieving a state of equilibrium, or homeostasis, optimizes our healing potential. Start by setting your state of consciousness at zero. Through life's trials and tribulations the emotion of anger, at some point, will settle in. Let's say your anger reaches a level of minus fifty (-50). There must be plus fifty (+50) of joy to balance out this energy field and return you to neutral or equilibrium *(see Figure 1)*.

Figure 1: Opponent Process Theory

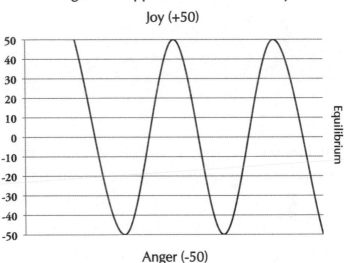

Joy (+50)

Anger (-50)

In a way, this balancing is an example of the Yin-Yang theory. The same is true with, for example, anxiety at a level of minus ninety (-90). There must be a level of calm that is capable of reaching plus ninety (+90) in order to balance out the energy field. Otherwise, the whole world would be experiencing and expressing an apparent inability to be joyful or calm. We know that fact to be *not* true.

To balance out your energy field when you are experiencing a negative emotion, first identity the negative emotion. Then, activate the opposite positive emotion by concentrating on thoughts which bring you the corresponding positive feelings. It is easier, for example, to get to a *joyful* state, rather than a *calm* one, when you're experiencing the toxic emotion of *anger* (joy is the polar opposite of anger). As the above sine curve shows, energy flows in waves up and down, capable of being either positive or negative. Remember "E-motion" is "energy" in motion. Joy is on the opposite side of anger, whereas calm is on the opposite side of anxiety.

So how does this apply to your life? When your partner is furious with something, don't tell him or her to "Calm down!" because calm will not counter anger. Instead, initiate some thoughts or actions that will cultivate joyfulness.

To understand this approach better, let's take a look at what someone might say to a spouse who is experiencing a high dose of seemingly uncontrollable anger. For example, imagine that a couple is traveling about forty-five mph down a back road on their way to a dinner party. The husband decides to take a shortcut to avoid traffic because he ran late at work and they are now about fifteen minutes behind schedule. Suddenly, a raccoon runs in front of the car and he has to hit the brakes hard, so as not to run over it. Meanwhile the car following them is not quite as quick and slams into them from behind. The husband's first reaction is, "Oh my God!" He is very angry. The wife says, "Calm down." The husband replies, "I'll be damned if I can calm down after what they've just done!" Meanwhile, nobody, including the angry husband, actually *wants* to be angry for more than a few moments—anger, as we feel it, is a very uncomfortable emotion to experience. So the challenge is to process the emotion and move on to a more positive state. The wife could initiate some thoughts or actions that she knows will bring her spouse the feelings of joy in order to counter the anger. They don't have to be the happiest things in the world, just on the way up the vibration scale to joy. She might say, "At least we're not injured! We're alive! And the car is basically fine. Remember when you backed into the stone wall last week and left a dent in the trunk? Now we can have the rear end repaired."

ESTABLISH EMOTIONAL STABILITY

One of the keys to developing emotional stability, wisdom and insight is expressing negative emotions and then consciously moving on to a more peaceful state. No matter how much pain and anxiety we are feeling, these emotions are a consequence of how we are perceiving our world. Pay attention to how you feel. If you are stuck in negativity, change your thought patterns. Shift your focus from the negative emotion to the countering positive emotion. When you feel angry, shift to thoughts of what brings you joy. When you feel anxious, shift to thoughts that make you feel calm. I am not providing examples of what those thoughts might be because what makes you feel joyful is not always what makes others joyful. The same is true for what is calming to you. We are all individuals.

Along those lines, when we feel scared, we know that not everyone in the whole world is scared. Some people may be scared when an earthquake erupts or when a hurricane is approaching and that emotion may seem overwhelming, but there are many other people acting out of courage and bravery during these trying times. Again, it is up to us to shift our thoughts to the positive polar opposite of whatever negative emotion we're feeling in order to alleviate the pain and imbalance associated with the negative emotion.

A few other examples of shifting our emotions to positive from negative include: acceptance is the opposite of frustration; clarity is the opposite of confused; and flexible is the opposite of stubborn. Think about some situations that would help bring you out of negative emotion. What are you more accepting of in your life when frustration abounds? What are you very clear of as far as direction in your life when you get confused? And how can you be more flexible when you realize you're being stubborn?

As we take responsibility for our emotional stability we will find that we are increasingly able to shift to thoughts of things, people or events that make us happy. As we continue on this path, we will start to embrace a belief system that builds genuine happiness. While we work to find the good and to shift from negative to positive emotional states, it's important to remember that we live within relationships— spouses, parents, children, siblings, friends, classmates, co-workers… Our changes will affect those who are close to us, who may be willing to make these changes as we do, or who may challenge us. Remember that we all need each other for continued learning and growing. Most of us need to cultivate a better understanding and appreciation for knowing we are all different, and that's a good thing! Cooperate and communicate by sharing views and beliefs that enhance each other's spiritual growth. We can make life and our relationships much more fulfilling by believing in ourselves, believing in each other, and being creative with our challenges. Most importantly, we must be patient and tolerant while being authentic with respect to our partners and to ourselves. In your own life, allow the positive energy to flow and transform you with the awareness that everything is love. And know that *love is expressing itself the best way it can under the circumstances.*

There will always be challenges in relationships. Our task is to look for ways to be more creative, to grow, and to allow for better and deeper ways of enjoying togetherness. We should not look at situations as hopeless, but as challenges that we are perfectly equipped to handle. Above all, we should not blame our negative emotions on our partner—we alone are responsible for our emotional state.

Be honest with yourself. If a romantic partner doesn't have a particular quality you want in a person, but has twenty-five other good qualities that you value, and you abandon the relationship, are you being realistic? It sometimes appears during emotional setbacks that the grass is greener on the other side. Remember, when you are entrenched and obsessed with negativity you should not make arrangements to escape. Make the shift and move to the polar opposite emotion. What makes *you* happy? Think about it... Now, feel it!

CHERISH VERSUS GRIEVE

Grief is a powerful emotion that almost all of us experience at some point. Grief may arise due to illness, the end of a meaningful relationship, the death of a loved one, losing a job, or moving away from a beloved home or city. Sometimes emotions are unwelcome, and grief often is. Grief can also be prolonged, causing emotional imbalance that in turn leads to physical symptoms. But while grief is a part of life, we do not need to develop life-threatening health conditions as a result of experiencing a tremendous loss. Instead, we can choose to acknowledge the grief and process it rather than live in it.

Let's consider the feeling of loss when a loved one dies. This feeling is grief, which we often internalize. Grief and sadness, according to Traditional Chinese Medicine, are emotions associated with the lungs. If we experience the loss of a loved one, often we will break down and cry with an uncontrollable gasping, which in turn can usher in a susceptibility to allergies, tightness in the chest cavity, and even shortness of breath.

Grief can also give rise to much more serious health issues when it goes unacknowledged and is repressed. Many visitors to hospital emergency rooms show up with chest pain and shortness of breath that is caused not by a heart condition, but by grief. I have a patient and dear friend, Dr. John Braden, who is the director of the emergency rooms at South Miami Hospital, Kendall West Hospital and Mariners Hospital in Florida. He is an excellent, compassionate, well-informed medical doctor. I once asked him if anyone ever came into the hospital emergency room with chest pain and shortness of breath, and after countless hours of evaluation and examination utilizing state-of-the-art medical equipment, his team found all tests to be within normal limits? Of course, he said, "Yes!" "So what do you do with these patients?" I asked. He answered, "The common medical approach, at this point in the visit, is to make sure they are stable. Then we refer them to the 'psych ward.' "

I proposed to Dr. Braden that he perform an experiment of sorts to explore how emotional imbalances can lead to physical symptoms. He agreed. My proposal was simply that over the course of a month, he add one question to his consultations with these patients: "Did you happen to lose a family member, close friend, or even a pet in the past couple of months?" The results were astonishing. Some of the patients looked at him as if he had psychic powers. The patients were immediately calmed and pleased to know, after a brief explanation, not only that they were not having a heart attack, but that they would overcome the symptoms with some quality emotional counseling and guidance during these difficult times as they grieved the loss of a loved one.

My aim in having Dr. Braden ask the question was ultimately to change how these patients are handled—my hope was that they would be guided more gracefully and efficiently through the emergency room and be reassured more quickly. And of course, I also hope that both doctors and patients develop a greater respect for the close relationship between our emotions and our bodies.

This is a simple example of the flow of qi (energy in the form of emotion) and how it can affect organ systems of the human body. These symptoms, when addressed only by Western medicine, can lead to unnecessary drug use or the embarrassment of an apparent "weakness," resulting in patients embarking on an expensive jaunt with psychological counseling.

When grief is the cause of chest pain and shortness of breath, a patient needs only build a healthy boundary to the emotion by gathering the proper tools, strategies and support for moving through the tragic experience. One very effective answer is The LifeLine Technique®—it is a way of harmonizing emotions that are negatively impacting us. Advice for those suffering from grief includes consciously moving to thoughts of cherishing time shared with the loved one instead of focusing on the separation. It is also very helpful to focus on what was learned from the loved one and ways to share that wisdom with others. This advice, along with The LifeLine Technique, has helped my patients who are emotionally overwhelmed by grief.

Processing the emotion involves a conscious awareness and must be practiced by each patient in a way that works for him or her. Each of us knows ourselves better than anyone else knows us, and if we are open to completing the life experience and regaining emotional stability when challenged with emotions like grief, we are our own best resource for getting back on track to well-being.

Conversely, when toxic emotions are dwelled upon and incorporated into daily perceptions, over time this leads to a surreal reality, one of impending doom. In order to master this game of life we must accept that we will experience pain, fear and challenges during the course of a lifetime. Being that the mind does not know the difference between imagination and reality, one can have a susceptibility to an illness or disease just by holding on to a particular negative thought pattern. Remember, if it's not a life or death situation, holding on to the feeling of FEAR could be holding on to *"False Evidence Appearing Real."*

GOOD LUCK

Create your reality by welcoming good luck into your life. Good luck is merely preparedness when opportunity arises. I tell my patients that we must overcome our challenges creatively instead of helplessly. So begin to set your table for luck and pull up a chair. Not feeling lucky lately? "Hard work, sweat and perseverance will often lead to good luck," according to my friend Frank Hawkins, who was quoted at the outset of this chapter. Those words of wisdom are from his first-hand experience.

When you are emotionally strong and stable, with a well-developed consciousness and awareness, you are able to harmonize negative emotions that otherwise might contribute to a weakness when you are faced with misfortune. None of us are exempt from life's difficulties—tragedies affect us all because we are all interconnected. One way or another we are affected by the disasters in this world. Hopefully, you personally are not feeling overwhelmed by negative emotions stemming from tragedies and difficult circumstances. But if you are, see this as your wake up call to get to work on yourself. This is *your* time. You owe it to yourself to live your own best life, and you owe it to the world. We are all interconnected and your inner peace and well-being are integral aspects of the whole universe.

Start with a daily practice to foster your inner peace and innate ability to be kind, which are important keys to cultivating happiness. Begin to serve your neighbor and give to your favorite charities. Live compassionately. Allow a shift to empower your intention and fulfill your dream of living in heaven here on earth. "It's always here and now!" says my friend Kelly Hostetler, a creative artist, poet and philosopher. This is *your* chance to live your very best life. As you increase your learning capacity, which is your willingness to learn and accept change, you begin to foster your innate ability to heal from any health condition. Begin realizing that you are powerful beyond your imagination!

Chapter Three

THE SCIENCE OF LIFE

Ayurveda is beyond beginning and ending. A science of eternal healing...a true teacher can teach one how to swim, but the swimming is up to the student...it is a lifelong journey.
— Charaka Samhita, Sutrasthana

Years ago I traveled to The Ayurvedic Institute in Albuquerque, New Mexico to take a course on helping people heal from psychological trauma. I studied with Dr. Vasant Lad, a leader in the world of Ayurvedic medicine. The word Ayurveda comes from the Hindu science of medicine and means "science of life." It is a holistic approach to health care and the practice of well-being that originated in India approximately five thousand years ago.

Ayurveda involves the practices of yoga, meditation and panchakarma. Panchakarma is a nutritional program designed to detoxify the body/mind. Yoga is actually a way of life and is much more than just moving through a sequence of asanas. Asanas are body postures designed to promote the flow of energy and blood and can be quite helpful in stretching or lengthening muscles and improving coordination and balance. I am not going to expound on the many forms and styles of yoga but highly recommend it as a healthy thing to do. In fact, practicing yoga compliments a decision to embark on a spiritual journey quite well.

Ayurvedic medicine addresses the challenges of disease and illness with the above-mentioned practices along with utilizing herbs and teas. I had a background in Ayurvedic medicine from earlier studies at the Chopra Center in Carlsbad, California, and this was an opportunity to learn more about healing from a different angle and from a highly respected authority of this ancient practice. The course was designed to increase knowledge regarding the emotional and mental doshas, or body/mind energy patterns.

While at the Ayurvedic Institute, Dr. Lad taught me the concept of *complete* and *incomplete* life experiences. The ultimate take home was that one develops wisdom when one consistently completes life experiences.

So, what is considered a life experience? Basically, it is an exposure to a situation that stimulates thoughts, feelings and action or expression. An incomplete life experience is when we have a thought that is relative to an experience, be it a relationship, task, project or challenge, and we then proceed to ignore the feelings associated with the thought. What happens thereafter is very common. The energy associated with the thought gets buried somewhere in our body/mind. This behavior is referred to as internalizing, and it is one of the ways we protect ourselves when we don't have the immediate ability to express how we really feel about something or someone.

To better understand how we develop wisdom by completing life experiences, I will explain how a life experience as a human being becomes complete. As this process is carried out and practiced, you will learn how wisdom unfolds.

Our *intellectual intelligence* originates in the frontal cortex of our brain. The frontal cortex is what we commonly refer to as our mind and it is located in the part of the cerebrum found deep within our forehead. The frontal cortex is where free will and reasoning are authorized. In kinesiology when we place an open palm over this part of our head we refer to it as our mind's reflex point.

Emotional intelligence is located in our heart. According to recent studies our heart is five thousand times more electromagnetically powerful than our brain. We should consult with it more often! The heart is the most powerful field generator in the human body. Dr. Paul Pearsall, in his book *The Heart's Code*, explains to us how the heart is not just a pump but also an epicenter of emotional intelligence. Gregg Braden's research, presented in his book *The Divine Matrix*, supports this theory. Our emotional intelligence is activated when we consciously put our hand over our heart and breathe.

When we bring our *intellectual intelligence (brain)* together with our *emotional intelligence (heart)*, notice where the two regions meet—right at the *throat chakra* region. I provide detailed information about chakras later in this chapter. But briefly, the throat chakra maintains the energy we access to speak our truth; it is where we harness the power to communicate.

When we take a moment to think, breathe and feel, our decisions to act in a certain way have access to a universal guidance. How do we know this? Because quantum physics proves to us that everything in our universe is interconnected and influenced by intention. By thinking, breathing and feeling we are *intentionally* taking a moment to tap into the collective consciousness. In turn, our expressions become acts we can trust and inherently become healthy choices.

There is an intelligence factor, called conscious energy, which substantiates our actions based on the collective consciousness and a universal truth. Remember though, not all our individual, personality-driven truths are alike. What is true for one person is not always true for another. There is one universal truth, however, that I like to teach, and that is: *everything is love expressing itself the best way it can under the circumstances.* John Lennon and Paul McCartney had something to say about this universal truth and put it this way in a song, "All You Need Is Love": "All you need is love, love. Love is all you need…"

COMPLETING LIFE EXPERIENCES

Sometimes thoughts never make it to the "feeling" mode. It's expression of "feeling" that completes a life experience as a human being. Let me repeat that. It's expression of "feeling" that completes a life experience. That completion is how we develop wisdom. We are all familiar with the detrimental effect created by storing up a multitude of incomplete life experiences. That state is called feeling overwhelmed. We are overwhelmed when we say things like, "I have no time for this," or "I don't want to go there," or "Let's put that on the back burner." These are all examples of things we say when we have a build-up of incomplete life experiences.

We can collect and store several hundred experiences without truly feeling them and expressing our truth. After all, we are pretty resilient. We complete life experiences by thinking, consciously feeling, and finally by going through the process of expressing the emotion. To better understand how to complete life experiences and make healthier choices I present the following real life example.

Let's say you are meeting with your financial planner. Your intention is to receive accurate information and act on the advice given to you. Your question: What is in your best interest for maximizing return with minimal risk? As you listen to your advisor's strategies regarding the investment at hand, you begin to formulate your own decision by taking a breath and being aware of all your senses. How do you feel? What happens at that moment in your existence? Do you hear something startling? Do you smell something strange? Do you suddenly get a weird taste in your mouth?

Now, change your strategy—think about your other investment options and repeat the breath and moment of awareness. Pay attention to your "being in the now." If you don't pay attention to the feeling or sensing aspect, you will start to rationalize and consequentially react by using thinking instead of feeling. That decision will be affected by rationalizations and the build-up of incomplete life experiences involving money matters. It can possibly distract you when it comes time to managing your money. The reason is that we are hard-wired, so to speak when it comes to money matters. Thoughts and feelings associated with money throughout our lives tend to trigger protective, survival or defensive modes.

Our responses to financial issues become habitual, almost instinctual, and most of us are unaware of these processes. If we don't learn to develop wisdom by practicing the process I described above, we succumb to feeling stuck and indecisive. That is one reason why many people find it impossible to build wealth. Consequently, those people are barely keeping their heads above water when it comes to finances and pay-ing bills.

How is it that we become overwhelmed by these incom-plete experiences, especially given that we're pretty resilient? The problems arise with the stockpiling of many incomplete life experiences and the consequences of avoiding the chal-lenges we need to face in life. We find ourselves saying things we really don't mean because we aren't fully present and re-sponding. Then we apologize ("I didn't mean to say that... I'm sorry.") We also may start beating ourselves up with nega-tive self-talk that we intend to be motivating: "I've got to get my act together," and/or "I've got to get focused! This project needs to be ready first thing tomorrow morning." We've all been there, right?

When we have too many incomplete life experiences we become overwhelmed, vulnerable, and do things and say things that get us into trouble. So take a moment when an important decision has to be made or when you are experiencing something that may feel uncomfortable. Complete the life experience by thinking, breathing and feeling, then respond accordingly.

THE SEVEN BASIC CHAKRAS

Many excellent and comprehensive books have been written explaining chakras, and anyone who wants to learn more about them has a multitude of wonderful resources from which to choose. In this book, I am going to limit myself to a brief introduction to chakras and an overview of how I have experienced their existence. I will also explain how I work to balance chakra energy fields with my patients.

Learning how the chakras function and how you can work with them yourself can be an extremely powerful self-healing tool. As I review the chakras, I include some basic but useful information concerning tools and ways to balance your own chakras.

The word *chakra* means "wheel" in Sanskrit. There are seven basic chakras relating to seven orbits of energy that encompass our bodies' front and back sides. Our chakras are *fields of energy* that contribute to the healthy function of organs and total body systems.

The concept of chakras helps confirm our human existence as a combination of body, mind and spirit. In a way, the study of chakras aids in our understanding that we are all interconnected. Chakras open and close depending on our ability to process our thoughts and express our emotions. I address chakras, as a holistic doctor, as access points to aid in the transfer of energy associated with completing life experiences—in other words, the expression resulting from the transformation of *thoughts* into *feelings*.

When chakras are out of balance the effect can be similar to a wagon wheel with a couple of missing rungs. The resulting weakness is subtle, yet palpable. The chakras also can specifically affect our hormone levels. According to Dr. Light Miller, a fellow Floridian and teacher of Ayurvedic medicine, "When our chakras are in balance we have maximum vitality and maintain an energy field prone to health and well-being. When our chakras are blocked we become vulnerable to feeling dull and sluggish." Dr. David Frawley, a highly respected authority on Ayurvedic medicine, teaches us that, "Each chakra provides an awareness of corresponding levels of the universe beyond the physical, where we can gain insights into the subtle workings of nature, life force, and the process of cosmic creation."

We have three lower chakras:

1. Root

2. Sacral

3. Solar Plexus

These three are located close together from the base of the pelvis to just above the belly button, and are associated with our physical nature and ability to stay grounded.

We have three higher chakras:

5. Throat

6. Third Eye

7. Crown

These three form the region of the neck and head as named and govern our ability to formulate expressions from the higher brain centers.

In the middle we find the epicenter of the seven chakras. It is where the three lower and three upper chakras meet:

4. Heart

Please remember that all seven chakras circumscribe and make up the fields of energy around our entire bodies (*see Figure 2*).

Figure 2: Human Energy Centers (Chakras)

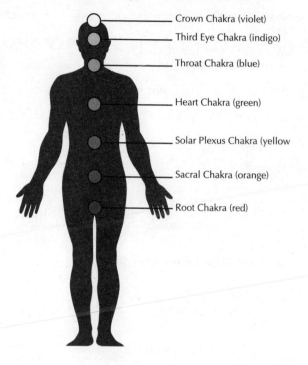

Although chakras are not physical by nature, they may be felt by the hands of someone trained in energy medicine or vibrational healing such as Reiki. You will be able to tell which of your chakras are in need of attention as you read the corresponding issues for each one. You also will be able to balance that chakra by activating your senses by using the color, scent, kinesthetic, and sound associated.

To treat the visual sense befitting each of the listed chakras you can imagine the color associated with it, or simply look at something depicting that color. Use the scents I recommend for balancing the appropriate energetic fields via the sense of smell. Hold the stone or mineral close to the appropriate part of your body when addressing the kinesthetic nature. The sounds or chants I present are very helpful, especially if you do not have the specially formatted and calibrated tuning forks designed to treat chakra dissonance. While activating all your senses with the provided tools, repeat the mantra "infinite love & gratitude" to balance and harmonize the chakra. We use this phrase because it is the universal healing frequency. There is quite a bit more involved in harmonizing chakras, but this is a great starting point.

THE 1ST CHAKRA – ROOT

Imagine yourself as a holographic display of this universe. Feel the power of one. The root chakra is all about our connectedness to Earth. Its energy is fortified by contemplating oneness and imagining the importance and purpose of your existence. Beginning around our pelvis and genital region is the root chakra. It is associated with the color **red** and the aroma of patchouli, frankincense or myrrh. To balance this chakra I have people put on red glasses and smell patchouli oil as we recite the words "infinite love & gratitude." Our bodies, which are made up of mostly water, will absorb the vibrations from the words "infinite love & gratitude," and our intention is to balance the chakra while the senses of sight and smell are activated. The mineral or stone to use for kinesthetic balancing is either black onyx or hematite. Hold the stone over the body region and say the words "infinite love & gratitude" to harmonize your sense of feeling—in essence this balances your awareness of the fact that you are grounded in your being here and now. The mantra to activate an audible vibration enhancement is "LAM," using the "ah" sound as in "Laaaaaaaahm."

Energy will leak from the root chakra when we experience powerlessness, insecurity and financial instability. Be aware of the beliefs you hold regarding money and/or family matters. They can either help or hinder your ability to stay grounded. Do your best to stay rooted in what you believe in and honor your family. Be respectful and polite without being judgmental of others. This can be a transcendental challenge.

THE 2ND CHAKRA – SACRAL

Issues regarding sexuality and sexual potency can be resolved by balancing the sacral chakra. Special attention should be paid to releasing control of situations that are out of your control.

The sacral chakra is located at the pubic bone around the body to the sacrum or the triangular bone at the base of the spine. It vibrates with the color **orange** and the scents of ylang ylang. Oranges or sandalwood may also be used for the aromatics.

The mineral or stone that vibrates in a similar frequency as the sacral chakra is orange carnelian. Sandstone or red jasper may be used as well. The tone used for balancing the sacral chakra is "VAM," using an "ah" sound as in "Vaaaaaaaahm."

The sacral chakra energy is associated with physiological functions of the genital region, the reproductive system, the urinary bladder and the small intestines. I often tell my patients to do their best to let go of jealousy and guilt, as these feelings tend to block energy from flowing through the sacral chakra. Be aware that stagnation of energy in this area can affect libido and sexual performance.

THE 3ᴿᴰ CHAKRA – SOLAR PLEXUS

The solar plexus chakra is named after the region from where our centering power or willpower originates. When energy is flowing through this region we may find it easier to embrace self-discipline. I learned this in 1980-81 while living with my Jeet Kune Do teacher, a Japanese American named Mike Jones. While studying this softer style of martial arts, which was developed by Bruce Lee, I learned how to channel my inner strength and determination by focusing on the qi (energy) in this area of my body.

The solar plexus chakra vibrates with the color **yellow** and is located between the belly button and the base of our sternum. If you hold a fist under the small, triangular shaped piece of cartilage called the xiphoid process in your midsection, you have found it. For aromatherapy you may use lemon, anise, juniper or rosemary. The stone or mineral one may choose is yellow citrine or gold for enhancing physical vibrations in the realm of self-trust and inner peace. The tone used is "RAM," using an "ah" sound as in "Raaaaaaaahm."

The pancreas, liver, stomach and adrenals can be affected when this chakra is blocked, so blood sugar levels and digestion can be compromised. On an emotional level, do your best to let go of beliefs that no longer serve you. This practice requires moments of self-reflection.

THE 4TH CHAKRA – HEART

The heart chakra is the center point of all seven chakras and mediates the energy flowing from the root chakra to the crown chakra. It is located over the chest region, directly over the heart, and between the shoulder blades of your back.

Focused heart chakra therapy helps one to realize that we are all interconnected. I like to remind my patients of

the Barbra Streisand song "People," with its famous lyr-
ics, "People who need people are the luckiest people in the
world." Do your best to realize that everyone and everything
in your life presents an opportunity to learn and grow.

The heart chakra vibrates in the color **green.** Aromatherapy
would include the scent of rose, bergamot, jasmine or cinnamon. The stone or mineral to use is green apophyllite,
malachite, or my favorite, rose quartz. You can use the tone
"YAM," using an "ah" sound as in "Yaaaaaaaahm" or the
mantra I learned at The Chopra Center, "Peace, Harmony,
Laughter, Love."

The heart chakra reflects emotional issues and is powered
by compassion and hindered by loneliness. When opened
and flowing, one can experience unconditional love with an
uncanny ability to know that everything is as it should be.

THE 5TH CHAKRA – THROAT

The throat chakra is involved, as you may have guessed,
with communication—speaking your truth and expressing
your feelings. Sore throats and upper respiratory problems
can arise when throat chakra energy is blocked or stagnant
from overly criticizing, judging or from frequent lying.

The throat chakra vibrates with the color **blue.** Aromas of
lyssop, sage, blue chamomile, lemon grass or tea tree can be
used to help this chakra to open and flow. The stones celestite,

turquoise and blue topaz are used for kinesthetics. Auditory stimulation is achieved by chanting the tone "HAM," using an "ah" sound as in "Haaaaaaaahm."

Physical issues could involve problems with the thyroid, parathyroid, vocal chords, TMJ (temporomandibular joint), mouth, teeth and/or gums.

THE 6TH CHAKRA – THIRD EYE

When our third eye chakra energy is flowing we seem to experience highly intuitive skills, enhanced intellectual capability, awareness and emotional stability. It is located between the eyebrows and is associated with the pituitary gland, a very important endocrine gland that runs the show, so to speak, with regard to the balance of hormones.

The color to use is **indigo** and aromatherapy oils such as peppermint, clary sage, eucalyptus, camphor, rosemary or basil can be used to help balance this chakra. The stone commonly used is amethyst, though azurite and lapis lazuli will work as well. The tone is "SHAM," again using the "ah" sound as in "Shaaaaaaaahm."

Unexplained headaches, dizziness and/or vision problems are sometimes due to third eye chakra imbalances, especially when neck vertebral fixations, blood pressure, low blood sugar, and hangovers from alcohol abuse have been ruled out.

THE 7ᵀᴴ CHAKRA – CROWN

The crown chakra is open when one is devoted to spiritual growth and self-actualization. The brain and the pineal gland, which is responsible for melatonin production, can be affected when energy flowing to this chakra is interrupted, leading to sleep disturbance. Dr. Light Miller warns us, "When energy associated with the crown chakra is blocked, we tend to dwell in the ego and pray out of desperation. In turn, we feel separated from God and our source."

The crown chakra is found at the top of the head and represents our connectedness to the divine. It radiates in the color **violet**. Frankincense, myrrh and lavender are commonly used in aromatherapy for opening this very important chakra field. We use clear quartz or clear crystal and the sound "OM" to help balance this chakra.

Now that you have a background in chakras and the fields of energy around us, I recommend you continue your education by getting started on the journey to experiencing divine grace. A great next step would be to read Caroline Myss' book *Defy Gravity*. In this book you will learn more about divine grace and how to experience *healing beyond the bounds of reason*. Caroline is an amazing woman, teacher, author and speaker. Check out all of her books. They are a wealth of invaluable information.

Chapter Four

BASE DECISIONS
ON "FEELING"

Coming back to America was, for me, much more of a cultural shock than going to India. The people in the Indian countryside didn't use their intellect like we do, they use their intuition instead, and their intuition is far more developed than in the rest of the world. Intuition is a very powerful thing, more powerful than intellect, in my opinion. That's had a big impact on my work.

— Steve Jobs, Co-founder and CEO of Apple, Inc.

Insight, or underlying truth, is based on intuition, feeling and wisdom. In our humanness we tend to disregard the value of accessing our innate intuitiveness when making decisions. Reasoning, sometimes called rationalizing, can back up any decision the ego puts forward. The art of rationalization has been mastered by politicians around the world. Not all, but many politicians are living proof that the mind will sometimes lie to the wisdom centers of the heart in order to substantiate righteousness. But why is it that we continue to deceive ourselves?

The characteristics of righteousness along with selfishness do not serve us well when it comes to building relationships. In order to build and nurture relationships in an intelligent and compassionate manner it helps to distinguish between thinking and feeling. We may find ourselves at times saying we *feel* something when we are actually *thinking* or *rationalizing* what have become programmed behaviors. The intention of this chapter is to enhance your ability to communicate with your inner self as well as with other people.

Communication is essential to developing a sense of personal contribution to this world. The ability to communicate, be it through words or body language, reconfirms to us that we are worthy of contributing our special talents and we are living a meaningful life. Awareness of self-worth and what we offer this world enriches our dignity and our faculty of integrity. Everyone has a special talent that they are born with. Along with that special talent comes the responsibility to share it. The most invaluable aspects of a special talent are bolstered by serving others. The acts of serving and sharing cultivate inner happiness. Let me say that again. *The acts of serving and sharing cultivate inner happiness.* Happiness comes from the awareness of your true self, of what makes you special. I recommend you do some self-reflection on what your special talent is and who you are. This type of contemplation can be a process for many people, and it's not always easy, but it's worth it. I will teach you how to ask yourself these questions on a daily basis when I provide tips on how to meditate in a later chapter. I cannot overemphasize how important this inquiry is—if you do not know who you are and what you bring to this world, you will not be able to access the inner core qualities that make perpetual happiness possible.

Know that your life is a *spiritual* journey that involves a *human* experience. Accepting this premise allows your attention to shift to learning what is presented in this chapter and throughout this book. My ultimate goal is to help you create true nobility. As defined by Dr. Wayne Dyer, true nobility isn't about being better than anyone else; it's about being better than *you* used to be.

"FEEL OUT" A SITUATION

The *mind* is the source of intellectual intelligence. It is a conglomeration of learned experiences and is shaped by personality. The *heart* is the epicenter of emotional intelligence. It is the place we need to focus on for guidance when we are making an important decision. When we give ourselves a moment to bring a thought into our heart, we can actually "feel out" a situation. The point is we can use our God-given gift of intuition (the sixth sense) along with our five senses: seeing, hearing, smelling, tasting and feeling, for making more conscientious decisions. When you are faced with a dilemma or an important decision to make, practice what I am about to teach you. This approach will facilitate your ability to speak your truth and honestly say, "Yes, I want more of that!" or, "No, thank you."

You were introduced to this technique when we talked about making financial decisions in the previous chapter. Put your palm over your forehead to activate the mind reflex point. Give yourself the recognition and understanding that you are thinking about something that requires a decision. Now put your other hand over your heart and take a deep breath. Ask yourself how you feel about this moment and the decision at hand. Whatever happens at this point, when you are consciously receptive to and looking for a sign from the universe, in other words, a feeling that guides you, your ability to act will be supported by an omnipotent power. The answer lies in your awareness at the moment you ask the question. How do you feel? What do you sense? Allow your senses to activate your innate guidance system. The answer will be guided by how you feel and through your awareness. When you are aware of anything and everything that happens at that point, no matter what it is, you can better formulate the appropriate response. Consequently, you will find yourself making better decisions with better results by doing what is called "following your heart."

Let's say, for example, that you are pondering whether or not to allow your teenager to go to a party with a friend. Right at that moment, you get an empty feeling in the pit of your stomach. Consider not letting her go. Or let's suppose that as you are practicing this technique for better decision-making, you suddenly hear a siren outside your home. Again, consider not letting your child go. They are signs from the universe, the place where you live. You are an intricate part of the universe. How about the option of letting her go, but insisting you drive her to the party? These are solutions attainable from the collective consciousness. It's okay for you to be cautious with your decision. This type of feeling out a decision is just one way I teach my patients to complement what already works for them. At the point of awareness, you can better formulate your decision based on factors such as past experiences with your child's friend, the friend's character and morals, and even the destination of the party.

On the other hand, when you ask yourself the question, then breathe and feel, if you get a feeling of calmness in your body and the look in your child's eye is trustworthy, then go ahead and let her go to the party. At that point stay in the realm of hope that everything will be okay and your child

will have fun and be safe. This is an example of how awareness and the practice of thinking, breathing and feeling can
help you, especially if you tend to worry a lot. This technique
can guide you with more confidence in the case of parental
decision-making.

Another example of what might happen right when you
are asking for a sign to guide you in your decision-making is
the wind blowing through the curtains and suddenly knocking over a vase. Imagine this happening. Right when you
ask yourself if you should let your teenager go to the party,
smash…the vase breaks. Lo and behold, you've got your answer! Sorry, the answer is *no*.

Having a little more fun with possibilities, let's explore
another scenario. You hear a cat fight outside your window as
you are about to make a financial decision. I am suggesting
you re-evaluate the investment. The universe has given you
a sign that the financial transaction you are about to make
could be complicated by temperamental hissing, scratching
and territorial whining. Is it worth it? Are you getting my
point?

Pay attention to *everything*. These are all signs from the
universe. Be conscious of the situation at hand. It may save
you a lot of aggravation down the road. This faith and belief
can help you make better financial decisions, as well as polish
your parenting skills.

The aforementioned examples help explain what is sometimes referred to as a "gut feeling." Know and believe that everything is interconnected. Decision-making is about having faith and belief not only in the universe but also in yourself. Practice "feeling out" a situation. The answers you get when you ask yourself "How do I feel?" will better guide you. Then the actions you make will facilitate inner peace, serenity and a better understanding of how the world works. Realize life does not have to be a struggle. You have options; you have choices. Know it. Believe it.

THOUGHT VIRUSES

According to doctors Richard Bandler and John Grinder, the founders and developers of NLP (neuro-linguistic programming), a thought virus is a "free-floating" belief in our system that we cannot link to a specific reference experience. In other words, we believe something without knowing why we believe it. Such thought viruses are often outside our awareness, even though they might strongly influence our behavior and decisions. Thought viruses are subconscious patterns that become ingrained in our being. They become activated as we are exposed to challenges we view as hopeless and when we are feeling helpless. So, who is responsible for this conditioning and programming? Who is spreading the viruses? Our teachers, parents, clergy and peers…that's who.

In other words, thought viruses arise from the perceived challenging experiences and happenings of growing up.

What if we are forced, by a mild form of temporary insanity, to disconnect from a thought? Or how about a time when you didn't have a strategy to express a thought or emotion and instead you internalized it? Perhaps your difficulty in verbalizing was due to perceived communicative barriers—in other words, you *were not able to express your hidden feelings.*

Maybe you have decided from past "learned" experiences that people cannot be trusted. There you were, dating the class valedictorian from an Ivy League school—and please note, this can apply to any promising romantic relationship, regardless of your partner's alma mater! Perhaps you were thinking something along the lines of, "Do I really deserve to feel this much love, this much joy…the potential for togetherness, stability *and* financial success?" Unfortunately, you may have bowed out of the relationship from the fear of being abandoned and hurt, when success was on the doorstep. Don't beat yourself up. You acted out of self-defense and self-protection. It wasn't a weakness. It *was*, however, a thought virus. You simply didn't, at the time, have the tools, strategies and support to stay connected to fulfill a dream. Be willing to "un-learn" what you have learned from your misfortunes or so-called "bad" experiences.

Thought viruses come in four different forms: *triggering, limiting, killer* and *Gemini.*

A TRIGGERING THOUGHT VIRUS

Triggering thought viruses can be activated when we are experiencing a situation that "triggers" a protective, aggressive or defensive response. If we are bombarded with triggering thought viruses we begin to live in a "cause-and-effect" world instead of creating our reality. Something happens and we end up acting out the same scenario time and time again. A wise man named Dr. Victor Frank once told me, "If you keep doing what you've always been doing, you're going to get what you've always gotten."

An example of a triggering thought virus would be if whenever someone cuts you off while driving, you immediately curse the other driver and perhaps even give them a nasty gesture. This leads to feelings of frustration, anger and what is known as road rage. This virus, which overcomes the mind, foregoes any etiquette training and dodges the diplomatic filter within your brain.

The subconscious reactive mind is then activated and responds inappropriately. Triggering thought viruses can escalate into arrogance and disrespect in social situations. For example, suppose you are disrespectfully cut off during a conversation and then you automatically respond in a cheeky, condescending manner. This is certainly not in your innate loving-kind nature, but a triggering effect occurred.

A LIMITING THOUGHT VIRUS

Limiting thought viruses are non-physical in nature. However, they *do* affect the whole body just like a cold or flu virus can. They cause symptoms like stomachaches or headaches, as do flu viruses, but they are derived from subconscious thought patterns. Limiting thought viruses, like their microscopic cousins—the cold and flu viruses, arise when we are vulnerable or overwhelmed. Viral "bugs" are opportunists in that they overtake the body when the environment is ripe for attack and the immune system is compromised.

Imagine you are a fourteen-year-young man and your baseball coach tells you after countless attempts at hitting curveballs, "Ah, forget it son, you'll never hit a curve ball!" Fast forward a few years and you are an extremely talented eighteen-year-old third baseman in college with an opportunity to try out for a major league team. What happens? You fail to impress the scout because you struck out six times in a row as you were thrown seventy mph curve balls. Meanwhile, in batting practice, you were hitting ninety mph fast balls out of the park. It wasn't that you couldn't hit a curve ball. It was that you *thought* you weren't able to because of a *limiting* thought virus. In this example a limiting thought virus affects the body's ability to overcome the conditioned belief of the mind. One very effective way to treat a limiting thought virus is to re-visit it, then clear or harmonize it using The LifeLine Technique.

Here's another example of a limiting thought virus. A seven-year-young girl struggles to finish her math homework. She's only in second grade and it's getting late in the evening. Her mom is going over her worksheet and finds she's got almost half the problems wrong and says, "Don't worry dear; you'll never be good at math. I wasn't, and neither was my mother. I believe it's in our genes. Let's go to bed." From that point on, it's possible this little girl will grow up believing she'll never be adept at mathematics. She may even suffer from math scores that hover around sixty percent, barely passing, and she may actually come to hate numbers, figures, algebra, geometry and accounting. She may miss all the fun with math, which I, personally, have found to augment problem solving. After all, with math, you know when you've got it right or not. It *is* an exact science. And when you get it, it's very rewarding and has applications throughout our lives, from creating budgets to calculating tips to financial planning.

We overcome challenges by being creative and by realizing there are infinite possibilities available to us in this world. As children, we begin the process of living on purpose and developing a sense of self-worth by realizing that we have the ability to succeed. This belief becomes an invaluable character trait when problems and challenges arise. Limiting thought viruses get in the way of growing and learning and can make life quite difficult. Thought viruses contribute to imbalances in physical health, which in turn can lead to medical diagnoses and treatment. This process sometimes can give rise to additional limiting thought viruses. For example, a physician can lead you to believe you have to be on a medicine for the rest of your life, or a chiropractor can lead you to believe you need to be adjusted every week for the rest of your life. But remember, anything is possible and you have options.

I was traveling in Southeast Asia in the summer of 2005 with my dear friend Dr. Darren Weissman, who is the developer of The LifeLine Technique®. While we were touring Bangkok, Darren decided to have his fortune told by an awesome-looking old Thai man. This wise-looking, yet frail, long-bearded source of ancient wisdom told Darren he would live a long, prosperous life and be a gift to those who knew him, learned from him, and followed him. All of this is true! Darren is now an internationally renowned holistic doctor, speaker, educator and best-selling author of *The Power of Infinite Love & Gratitude*.

Besides being incredibly accurate with his palm reading and his use of the Chinese calendar wheel, he proceeded to tell Darren he would die around the age of eighty-four, to which Darren immediately proclaimed "Wow! I'm going to clear that limiting thought virus right now!" We both had a good laugh afterwards and moved on to tour Bangkok's Grand Palace.

A KILLER THOUGHT VIRUS

Killer thought viruses are a combination of multiple triggering and multiple limiting thought viruses. They are responsible for acts of suicide and severe depression. They literally program a person into living in death modes. Killer thought viruses lead to complete breakdown of the bodily systems that are designed to protect and cooperate in a holistic manner. They are often associated with the cause of cancer and they must be detected and harmonized or cleared to allow for a shift into the awareness that "life has meaning."

Like other thought viruses, killer thought viruses can be harmonized and cleared by using The LifeLine Technique. If untreated, cells invaded by a killer thought virus can move from anaplasia to dysplasia and finally present themselves as cancer cells. After harmonization and clearing of a killer thought virus, these same cells can progress into healthy cells. After all, it's in their nature to be healthy!

The cells in our bodies have always maintained an ability to regenerate healthy, vibrant living tissues. It's just our conditioned minds that succumb to the accelerated degeneration we see so often. The fact is, all humans have the ability to live to be ninety to one-hundred-plus years of age. Sometimes we find ourselves believing in the limiting thought virus of: "I probably will die around age seventy-five, because both my father and grandfather died at that age." Talk about digging your own grave at such a young age these days. Personally, I'm thinking, "Wow, I've reached fifty years of age. I'm so happy I've still got half of my life left to live, love and laugh!"

A GEMINI THOUGHT VIRUS

Gemini thought viruses are examples of times when we think we need to be someone else in a certain situation or when we are feeling like we need to hide our true selves due to the pressure of compromising circumstances. This is where shame and guilt perpetuate. Gemini thought viruses can be likened to a clown who is wearing a painted face of a huge smile but deep down inside he feels very sad.

This is when we struggle to accept who we are and in turn portray who we think we should be. In effect it reveals fakeness about us. When we are not able to embrace ourselves, others will likewise find us unappealing. To overcome Gemini thought viruses, we must embrace all sides and all parts of ourselves, both the positive and negative.

One of the most respected, brilliant teachers of Indian Ayurvedic medicine is Dr. Deepak Chopra. He has taught me many things. One of the more profound concepts he professes is, "If you were to pick out ten characteristics of someone you really admire and then ten characteristics of someone you really despise…know that you are a combination of all of these twenty traits!" If you don't possess those ten traits you despise in others, you would never have the awareness to pick them out in the first place!

It is when we become aware of the negatives that we create the opportunity to consciously choose to change. This is when we can appreciate contrast of character and act to better ourselves.

One of the most spiritually enriching books I have read is *The Eye of the I: From Which Nothing is Hidden* by David R. Hawkins, M.D., Ph.D. We all know when we are trying to fool ourselves or when we rationalize by talking ourselves into or out of something. When this happens we are parasitic or vulnerable to Gemini thought viruses. Remember, Gemini thought viruses are the cause of a projected smile on your face, even when you are feeling depressed inside.

Universally, we choose to be happy and want to get better—we want to *feel* better if we are feeling bad, and we want to *get* better at anything that is difficult for us. Granted, it is much easier to get better at what we are already good at. But the concept of work comes in when we realize we need to improve one of our weaknesses. Choose to be patient and peaceful. Choose to be fair. *And always, always choose LOVE.* I recommend you watch the video "I Choose Love" at the website of my friend and fellow Certified LifeLine Technique Practitioner Shawn Gallaway: www.ShawnGallaway.com. It's worth your time. Share it with a friend.

STOP BLAMING THE WORLD

I have a patient I'll call Maria. She constantly tells me how happy she would be if only *this* would happen or if *that* could change along the lines of: "If I only had millions of dollars I would be happy," and, "If he could only change his messy habits I could feel at peace." Are you familiar with the world of *this or that*? If so, you are living in a cause-and-effect world like Maria, just waiting to put out another fire or looking to somehow escape the perils of life. This is classic avoidance behavior instead of what we call "creating your reality." You are running away from pain and sorrow instead of moving through challenges and moving toward light and levity.

First of all, happiness is within you all the time. You only need easy access to it, which is achieved by simplifying your life and shedding the ego. Secondly, peace of mind is always available when you filter the mind chatter and take care of *your* own business. As the singer-songwriter Jack Johnson points out, "Everybody's worried about everybody else." Let go of the need to know what everyone else is doing, what you expect of everyone else, and what everyone else expects of you. Have you heard of the "keeping up with the Joneses" syndrome? It's not really a medical diagnosis. I just made it up, but are you catching my drift? Start making the shift. Honor thyself.

Maria tells me every week how difficult life can be. She reminds me of all the turmoil in the world and fills me in on how bad people are. Unlike Maria, I don't watch the news on TV often, which is inundated with negative reports worldwide. I don't need to be reminded every day that there are car bombings in the Middle East, or that there are children starving in Ethiopia. I do not ignore these tragedies and misfortunes, I just choose to be the best I can be in my situation and support those who are in position to help make a difference. *I choose love.*

I am grateful to choose love and for the opportunity to coach Maria on how to do it. Whenever she comes to me for help I first ask her to set an intention, and the only rule is that it be something she is moving towards, not away from. I remind her that Ghandi would never join a "fight against war," but would lead a "movement for peace." Mother Teresa would never be involved with a "war on hunger," but would be the first to lead a "feed the hungry" program. What are you moving towards? What are your intentions for developing true nobility? Take responsibility for your own life and become better than you used to be at staying aware, mindful and healthy.

Chapter Five

RANDOM ACTS
OF COMPASSION

*The self-controlled person, moving among objects, with his
senses free from attachment and malevolence and brought under his own control, attains tranquility.*
— Bhagavad Gita

Nobody in their right mind wakes up in the morning and
says, "Today, I am going to be angry…all day!" Nor does
anyone in their right mind arise with the desire to worry all
day, but we see it happening to our loved ones and perhaps
ourselves. As you know, anger and worry are both toxic emotions. The reason people feel buried in toxic emotion, for
what may seem to be days or weeks or even longer, is because
they are stuck in subconscious patterns and are thrown into
survival modes—patterns of protection and defense.

In the summer of 2007, I was studying under Dr. Vasant Lad, a highly esteemed teacher of Indian Ayurvedic Medicine, with the goal of learning how to better help people overcome psychological traumas. I asked Dr. Lad, "How long should someone allow a negative emotion to linger in order to complete a life experience?" When I asked this, I was really wondering, "Why do some people stay angry so long?" Dr. Lad snapped his fingers and said, "Should be only that long. You feel it, express it with respect to yourself and the other party, then let it go!" Now, I know this sounds a lot easier than it is, but as you practice awareness you begin to realize just how stubborn one can be.

My friend Mimi Greek recently taught me another technique for completing life experiences I would like to share with you. In order to gain insight and wisdom from completing life experiences, allow a negative emotion to simmer within your mind and body for a full seventeen seconds without allowing more thoughts to feed the mood. It is common for people to contemplate anger, anxiety or fear, and support these feelings with outside thoughts and past events. Seventeen seconds of feeling without augmentation allows for total completion of that particular experience while not perpetuating the negativity associated with it. The more we learn to complete our life experiences, the more easily we can access wisdom.

I have a patient named Arla who has difficulty sleeping. She started seeing me for neck and shoulder pain. She was at the peak of menopause and doing her best to stay sane with all the physiological changes going on in her body. She also suffered from stomach issues such as bloating and indigestion. On top of all that, her bouts of insomnia were fed by incessant mind chatter, making it nearly impossible for her not only to fall asleep but also to stay asleep all night.

Arla worries about her brother, who constantly calls her and is always in need of money. She is saddened by her daughter's troubled marriage, and she is angry at her son-in-law, who emotionally abuses her daughter. Arla also struggles with anxiety brought on by her husband's health. He is battling prostate cancer.

When she first started seeing me, Arla's world was overwhelming to her and she had difficulty finding peace of mind. I began working with her by assuring her that she was in the right place and that I would help her. She needed to get back on track to feeling happy, peaceful and of course, healthy.

The first step was to help her recognize that overall she was a fairly healthy fifty-four-year-young woman. She is a personal trainer and actually practices what she preaches. I confidently proclaimed that once she realized that the universe would not deal her a hand she could not play, I would coach her on how to resolve the problems affecting her health, including how to support her husband so he could better heal and move past his experience with cancer.

The LifeLine Technique came in handy as a way to harmonize Arla's worry, anger and anxiety. I started Arla on a blend of the following herbs, which have proven to be quite helpful for women going through menopause. They are: black cohosh, chasteberry, dandelion, dong quai, wild yam, motherwort, licorice and ashwagandha. It is a very effective and popular formula with my female patients. Full spectrum digestive enzymes helped relieve her abdominal bloating and the herbs Magnolia officinalis and Ziziphus spinosa helped calm her at bedtime.

I also gave Arla tips on how to prepare for a restful sleep. Use these tips to support your own nighttime habits if you are having trouble sleeping. Start by brewing a cup of Yogi brand Bedtime Tea. It is a combination of herbs and spices for calming the mind and body. The key ingredients are valerian root, passion flower, St. John's wort leaf and organic chamomile. Licorice, cardamom and cinnamon are added to the blend to make for a delightful and relaxing beverage before bedtime. I instructed Arla to fill a basin of hot water and put it in front of her favorite chair. She then was to place her feet into the basin for ten to fifteen minutes so that the hot water would pull down the qi created by all the activity in her mind. If you would like to try this at home, it's a good idea to have a towel to put alongside of the basin for when you take your feet out. I learned the "hot water basin" technique from Dr. Fu Di, a sixth-generation doctor of Traditional Chinese Medicine at the University of Miami. This simple practice has helped many of my patients.

Follow this routine each night while listening to light classical music for about thirty minutes before going to bed. The idea is to prepare the body and mind for sleeping. It becomes a personal ritual you look forward to. However, this ceremony is not easy to perform or as effective when there are hundreds of incomplete life experiences on the mind; nor is it easily done after watching the television show *Criminal Minds* or the local news. Remember that incomplete life experiences are thoughts that never make it to the feeling and expression modes.

Step two is to consciously tell your body that it is time for a restful night's sleep. After washing your face and brushing your teeth, calmly crawl into bed, lie down and begin reciting a gratitude list. It can be aloud to your partner or simply in your mind. This is a list of eight to ten things you are thankful for what happened that day. If you get stuck trying to think of eight things, use a few simple ones like, "I am so thankful for this bed," "I am thankful for this opportunity to rest my mind," and "I am grateful to be alive." By allowing thoughts like this, you create a frequency that flows through the mind and body. And wouldn't you know, gratitude is a universal healing frequency! Pleasant dreams are in your future when you practice this routine.

THE FOUR SUBLIME STATES

Buddha taught us four sublime states to strive for in order to attain inner peace and true happiness. Practice showing and acting out of these four states. They will keep you emotionally stable and on the path to enlightenment. The four states are:

1. Loving-kindness

2. Appreciative Joy

3. Compassion

4. Equanimity

The first action to practice daily is *loving-kindness*. *Karma* is a Hindu word that means action. When we seek to create good karma for ourselves we must "act" accordingly. What we give, we receive. So if you "want" for example, more money, "give" more money to a worthy charity or to those in need. Remember, money is called "currency" for a reason; don't hoard it, it was created to flow. If it is more love you wish to feel, show more love to your fellow human beings. Should you feel the need for more time to share your special talents, donate some of your precious time to a non-profit organization. To be an example of a loving-kind person in your community will, in turn, bolster your own ability to find inner peace. Bottom line, be kind!

Secondly, show *appreciative joy* for any and all life experiences day in and day out. It has been proven countless times that *love* and *gratitude* are the universal healing frequencies in order to heal from any health concern. Whether it be heartburn or cancer, one must continually enrich oneself with thoughts and actions that are congruent with love and gratitude. Before you rise in the morning and when you lie down to rest at night, tell yourself how grateful you are for all people and situations in your life right now. Remember, thoughts have frequencies that run through your body so create an environment for perpetuating feelings of love and gratitude…This is a universal healing frequency!

The third very important sublime state is *compassion*. Do your best to practice taking away suffering from all living things. While you're at it, start to practice the ancient noble Hindu process of *Ahimsa*, which perpetuates life. Ahimsa is showing acts of kindness, love, appreciation and compassion for all sentient beings. This means: Stop killing things! I began this practice years ago and was astonished by the following personal observation. One day I walked into my bathroom and saw a line of ants running diagonally up the wall, in perfect formation, as if led by a strict Army battalion sergeant. Hundreds of tiny ants were mysteriously clinging to the wall and marching upwards, continuing along the junction of the wall and ceiling, and proceeding out a crack in the corner of the room, exiting to the attic. I connected, as best I could, to the concept of all living things being one and asked them to kindly leave. I told them, both verbally and mentally, "Please go back outside where you belong." I said to them, "Don't make me get drastic and call the exterminator. You belong outside. You are not welcome in this house. I will be back in one hour and you'd all better be gone!" Wouldn't you know it? When I returned, there was not one ant to be found. And they never returned! What I did was tap into a collective consciousness through thoughts and added a verbalization just to satisfy myself on a human level. I asked the universe to provide this action so that I could continue respecting all living things. It worked! It takes belief. Trust that we are all interconnected. Be patient, and by all means, practice tolerance.

To achieve the fourth and most sought-after sublime state, that of *equanimity*, or peace of mind, one must practice and achieve the first three states consistently. Attaining equanimity is achieved through the preparation for and the discipline of meditation.

LEARN TO MEDITATE

There is a silence or a pure positive awareness that always exists in our minds, but it can be drowned out by all the mind chatter of our busy days. Here are some tips to get started on a journey to inner peace.

Get ready to feed your soul and enrich your spirit. It is best to set aside thirty minutes each morning to meditate, preferably at sunrise. Each morning as you get up, go to the bathroom to pee, wash your hands, and splash some water onto your face. Proceed to blow your nose to clear your breathing passages and then head directly to your prepared sanctuary. Burn some incense to help create an atmosphere. You may choose to play music without words or maybe CDs especially produced for meditation, but I recommend total silence. Get used to entering a state of pure positive awareness.

Sit upright on a pillow either in lotus position (cross-legged) or in a comfortable chair facing east. We face east, if possible, out of respect for the Asian philosophy and teachings from which we learn this practice. Also, facing east serves to welcome the sunrise, which brings us light and warmth each day. Place your hands palms-up on your thighs. Bring the index finger and thumb of each hand together in a circle.

Take a deep breath...Now let it out. Start by chanting "OM" three times. Then, ask yourself these three questions:

Who am I?

What is my purpose?

What do I want?

Allow for a minute or so between each question. Listen for your mind to connect to thoughts/answers, which may vary during each stage of your life.

Now sit in silence for the next twenty-five minutes if possible. Each time a thought arises, let it flow, then let it go… Bring your focus back to your breath. If, for example, the tune "Hotel California" comes to your mind, simply sing it out…"Welcome to the Hotel California…Such a lovely place…Such a lovely face…" No need to keep going after that first stanza. The point is, don't try to stop the thoughts, but re-center yourself by repeating a mantra such as, "infinite love & gratitude," or, "peace," "harmony," "laughter," "love," or…create your own! A mantra will help you to regain your focus on breathing and what you are doing…you are meditating. Even the most seasoned and wise people who have been meditating for years have thoughts that pop into their minds. The process of meditating does not block thoughts from entering the mind. The idea is to increase the gap between your thoughts in order to rest the mind.

It takes discipline to meditate. Have a strategic plan for the optimal time and place. Concentrate on the pure silence between each thought. Sometimes colors will appear. Sometimes beaches, oceans, fields or stars in the nighttime sky. You will enjoy this place of pure potentiality.

When you are ready to come out of meditation, give your body a sign, such as wiggling your toes or opening and closing your hands. Bring your hands into a prayer pose. Bow your head. Thank yourself for the practice of meditation. Say *Namaste* (aloud or to yourself), which in Sanskrit means, "The spirit in me respects the spirit in you." Then open your eyes and get ready to enjoy your day! Look for the good in every encounter. Be kind, smile, love, and be loved...

During your meditations you will truly begin to appreciate the gaps between your thoughts. Remember, meditation is a much-needed break from the sixty thousand to eighty thousand thoughts we have each day! Be persistent. You can do it!

PLEASURE VERSUS PAIN

Besides hunger and satiation, there are two basic sensations that flow through our bodies each and every day—*pleasure* and *pain*. Too much pleasure will lead us down the road to addiction. Too much pain tends to lead us into emotional suffering. So where is the happy medium? Certainly not avoidance. If you are one of those people who says, "I don't feel anything," you are giving up wonderful opportunities to develop wisdom and insight.

PLEASURE

I get a lot of *pleasure* out of playing golf with my wife, Susan. The game of golf, like the game of life, holds many mysteries and has many lessons to teach us. Let's take the example of hitting a golf ball. As an exercise, I will compare a golf swing to life's challenges. When facing life's challenges we must be physically and mentally nimble and progressive. Similarly, a sound golf swing must be athletic and flowing.

The Address

When a golfer is able to address the ball with a solid foundation, present-time consciousness and the desire to be successful, he or she is envisioning and anticipating a good shot. As you begin to swing a golf club, the take-away should be focused and coordinated. The grip on the club should be aligned and firm, yet relaxed. Has anyone ever told you to "get a grip" on life? To get a grip means to be present, aware, focused and confident. Be aligned with your vision and be grounded in your decisions.

The Swing

As you reach the top of your backswing there should be no swaying. This is not the time to be wavering or indecisive. In other words, finish what you've started and envision successful completion of the project at hand. With a clear, focused mind there will be little distraction. Attention should be directed towards what is necessary for success. So the lesson here is: Get a grip on life and stay focused. Be aware that visual imagery and "feeling" create your reality.

A well-executed golf swing insures optimal distance and accuracy. A calm, focused approach to both the golf swing and life's challenges will generate feelings of confidence. Understand that focus, persistence and determination are the keys to success.

The Finish

You are moments away from a smooth, balanced finish, with hands held high in jubilation. The gratitude you have earned fills your heart and soul. No need to yell "Fore!" as your shot is right on target. You only have a ten-foot birdie putt to sink for exclusive rights to happiness and fortune. Sometimes this is the hardest part, but stay focused, you can make it! Remember, that ten-foot putt will be the finishing touch or the icing on the cake. Should you be able to accelerate through the healthy boundary you created with a steady head, you will win the game (of life).

Now, let's reapply those principles to life. As you begin a new project, start with a sense of desire and envision a successful outcome. You may be led astray with negative thoughts or past bad habits. Remember to still your mind by practicing meditation daily. Use the meditation tips from earlier in this chapter—they will serve you well. You must remain confident and focused, moving toward your goal throughout all stages of the project. As you make contact with people and situations, your innate ability to successfully work through and complete projects will be enhanced by hope and vision. The more you approach life in this way, the better you will get at mastering it.

Practice makes permanent your ability to rise to the occasion and overcome challenges. Trust in your abilities. Stay focused. Activate your senses—they are your own built-in guidance system. Have faith in yourself. Now, that was fun!

P.S. You made the putt. You won! Allow yourself to *feel* happy and grateful.

PAIN

Pain is your body's way of telling you something is not right with your current lifestyle and possibly with your views on life. Something needs to change. Be persistent in exploring what changes need to be made in order to reduce feelings of pain and embrace feelings of pleasure. You know your body better than anyone else does. You know what feels good to you. You know what's on your mind better than anyone else. When dealing with pain, try different approaches. Let yourself be coached, use various strategies, and find the right tools that empower you to make the changes necessary to get back on track to feeling good. Welcome the pleasure that comes from inner peace and tranquility. You know what feels good, what makes you happy, and what brings you pleasure. Welcome back to wellness.

Now, pick a number from between one and ten... Don't continue reading until you have whispered a number to yourself.

The number you came up with is the number of things you need to write down on paper. These are your wishes, dreams and circumstances that contribute to building genuine happiness. And, in essence, these are things you want to continue to manifest and become grateful for. These are persons, situations and events you are passionate about in life. Write them down; don't just store them in your memory. This is your gratitude/wish list. Read it often, especially before bedtime. Cherish the opportunities to make decisions that will help you realize these life experiences.

As you concentrate on these elements you will create a frequency throughout your body that brings you peace, pleasure and tranquility. This is a technique I recently used on my young son to help him fall asleep soundly at night. It has worked brilliantly! He now comes up with six things at bedtime that he is grateful for each day. It helps him get into the vibration of infinite love & gratitude, which is the perfect healing frequency for sleeping, rest and relaxation. Additionally, this frequency facilitates cell growth and repair. This exercise will alleviate the pain of emotional suffering brought on by doubts and fears. Practice it and be patient. The shift will come.

PATIENCE IS A VIRTUE

Along with meditation, it's a good idea to cultivate the virtues of patience and tolerance in your life. Have you heard the saying, "Patience is a virtue"? It is a proverb that has been taught for centuries by the great systems of wisdom in this world for a reason. In order to pleasantly go with the flow of life and see the world with a cup-is-half-full attitude, we must behave according to the wisdom in this proverb.

"Tolerance" in the Chinese character (忍) is symbolized as the edge of a blade (刀) on the heart (心). Why? This image represents how painful it is to accept others as they are while attempting to gently teach peace and loving-kindness through our actions.

A great wisdom of Buddhism says that those who have a tremendous reserve of patience and tolerance also enjoy easy access to calmness and tranquility in their lives. People with these qualities are more emotionally grounded, experience less illness, sleep with a clear conscience, and possess a genuine happiness.

We must do our best to bring patience and tolerance to consciousness so we are better equipped for making healthier decisions in life. It is times when our patience is tried that we must choose to be calm rather than selfish or defensive. Consciousness and awareness work best in overcoming the protective, defensive modes we are sometimes prisoner to. Meditation helps strengthen our reserves of patience. It behooves us to exercise our ability to embrace life with the attitude of gratitude, which is a patience-booster.

The practice of patience, tolerance and awareness also helps prevent over-developing of the ego. The ego does not need more developing in most people. It sometimes works overtime and creates quite the imbalance in our lives. The ego is an internal force which drives selfishness. It stands for "Edging God Out." Think about it.

SELF-LOVE VERSUS SELFISHNESS

Expression of love is a worthy practice, whether it is towards yourself, your pets, your car, your house or other people. However, there is a thin line between self-love and selfishness. Self-love is practiced when we take action in the five basics of healthy living. These are the quality, quantity and frequency of:

1. Water

2. Food

3. Rest (both of mind and body)

4. Exercise

5. Maintaining present time consciousness (staying in the NOW)

Selfishness is when one cares only about him- or herself and acts only for his or her own benefit while disregarding others. It is the opposite of compassion, in which we are in full awareness of someone else's well-being. Acts of compassion create the force that holds the universe together. So do your part to keep our world intact, turning and evolving. Learn to recognize when you are being selfish and call yourself out. Relinquish your need to be better than anyone else, unless you are competing to win a sporting event. Develop your true nobility. Remember, it's not about being better than anyone else. It's about being better than *you* used to be!

Selfishness is a seedling within all of us analogous to the existence of weeds in a garden of love. If you are feeding the weeds instead of tending to the fruits of loving-kindness and compassion, the weeds will choke you to death and prevent blossoms capable of thriving into a multitude of joys.

If you continue to be selfish, it will become a habit in which you perpetuate loneliness and actually create a callous wall around your heart. Remember, the heart is where we gather the emotion of joy. Counter selfishness and nourish loving-kindness by remembering that the heart mantra is "peace, harmony, laughter, love." Say it often and begin to open your heart to serving others and experiencing more joy.

Chapter Six

FIVE ELEMENTS THEORY OF TRADITIONAL CHINESE MEDICINE

Out beyond ideas of wrongdoing and rightdoing,
there is a field. I'll meet you there...
—Rumi

THE FIVE ELEMENTS

Traditional Chinese Medicine gives us what is known as the five elements theory to help us better understand the flow of qi and the flow of life. Presumably, the theory is about how to accept and appreciate change. The five elements theory presents us with an opportunity to reconnect to concepts associated with fire, earth, metal, water and wood. By learning the concepts that arise from the five elements theory, we can better shape our behaviors and more consistently perform acts of self-love.

The five elements are: Fire, Earth, Metal, Water and Wood.

FIRE

The element of *fire* reveals to us the modus operandi for living a passionate, fun and exciting life. Fire is a source of rising energy to keep us enthusiastic and stimulated to learn and grow. The positive emotions associated with fire are joy and happiness. The Big Bang Theory, what can be likened to a giant explosion or ball of fire, helps us better understand the formation of this beautiful, breathing planet Earth. As we explode inside, our passions generate energy in the form of self-expression, and our passionate expression (our personality) spreads enthusiasm. Both our energy and our enthusiasm are capable of enlightening everyone who comes into contact with us.

EARTH

The element of *Earth* reveals the challenging issues of self-worth and self-trust. When we are focused on what we *don't* want, instead of what we *do* want, we tend to become overwhelmed with anxieties and worries. There develops an intense wanting for things to be different. This whirling sense of longing leads to the depths of hopelessness sooner or later. One of the secrets to building genuine happiness is simply being happy with what you already have. Imbalances in our Earth element lead to feelings of guilt or shame. Guilt and shame are a result of living by someone else's values.

We sometimes refer to our beautiful planet as Mother Earth. Take a moment to connect in your mind to the unconditional love of your mother. Thank her for bearing you and all she did to the best of her abilities to bring you to life, teach you and feed you. Having a mother is one of the only things we all have in common on this planet, so let's honor our mother and forgive her for the times she may have been overwhelmed with stress and was unable to provide us with everything we wanted. Forgive her human foibles, just as you forgive your own. Accept her for who she is and recognize she did the best she could under the circumstances. You will be enriched by the thoughts of her and by recognizing that we all have unique histories. At this point in your life, if your mother has not been all that you wanted her to be, at the very least this exercise will be a virtuous step towards accepting and forgiving her. This is also a healing practice that will nourish your heart and soul, and help keep you balanced and grounded on this magnificent planet we call Earth.

METAL

The *metal* element helps us tap into the characteristics of strength, durability, flexibility and longevity. Metal reminds us to be bright and shiny, which means to be smart and project a fun-loving, light-hearted attitude. Our immune system is linked to this element, so nurture your understanding of the concept of bending but not breaking. Viruses and bacteria will be opportunist when we are rigid and rusting with dogmatism.

Imagine the steel girders that hold up the skyscrapers in cities. They are strong by nature and exemplify the hard work and determination of a team. It took a lot of planning and organization to build structures that provide an environment for the workplace while contributing to the maturation of civic identity in conjunction with the surrounding buildings. In this world, we all need each other to thrive. Urban planning, architecture and landscape architecture help bring more meaning to life on earth. Be grateful for the ways in which our man-made environment is designed and fostered. Notice and give credence to these aspects of community life. There are as many different types of buildings, architectural wonders and enchanting parks to enjoy, just as there are many different types of people.

The flexibility property of metal tells us to be open to what others have to contribute. When we are influenced by a hardened prejudice we are closed off from others and unable to embrace life—in this state, we inadvertently resist change. The characteristics and behaviors I am describing are warning signs telling us to let go and become more flexible with our views of what we consider right or wrong.

Rumi's mystical poetic verse states this eloquently:

> *Out beyond ideas of wrongdoing and rightdoing,*
> *there is a field. I'll meet you there.*

He goes on to say:

> *When the soul lies down in that grass,*
> *the world is too full to talk about...*
> *even the phrase "each other" doesn't make any sense.*

Be less judgmental and let go of your dogmatic tendencies. Breathe new life as you become more aware of the benefits of accepting others' individuality and how we can cooperatively embrace each other's uniqueness. As we learn to accept others, we can truly appreciate our differences. As you become more accepting you start to be attracted to more and more people. Consequently, you welcome fresh, new relationships that help you learn and grow and ultimately feed your bliss.

WATER

There is nothing on this earth that flows like *water*. When we think of the water element and what it can teach us, we need to acknowledge a sense of flow in daily life. Think about a tall cylindrical glass of water filled to the brim. Now, pour that water into a shallow bowl. If we look at the three-dimensional shape the water has taken, it now resembles a welcoming smile. The point is that it is the same water, just a different shape. This is a mental and visual lesson in authenticity. Water is true to itself; it adapts and flows like we do. Remember the explanation of a Gemini thought virus? Be yourself and act out of respect for yourself and those in your presence. There is nothing more beautiful in a human being than his or her ability to be authentic.

If you find yourself battling life's challenges and constantly paddling upstream, know that there are many ways to achieve success. Imagine that just a bit further upstream you can see an alluring waterfall with a gentle mist, creating a marvelous rainbow as the sun's rays reflect off the microscopic droplets. There is a soft breeze, birds are singing in harmony, and you are ready to bathe in the tantalizing waters just under the waterfall. You continue to paddle, and paddle and paddle but cannot seem to get there. It's time to reconsider your options.

Are you stubbornly holding onto old ideas? Are you feeling powerless and unable to focus because of exhaustion? Are you experiencing a lost sense of dignity? Well, here is your opportunity to release and move on. Paddle to the shoreline. Get out of the boat. Walk to the waterfall. When you keep doing what isn't working, you are only setting yourself up for blame and annoyance, which arise from rigidity. In other words, do something different.

Reconnecting in your mind to the properties of water allows you a few moments to settle down and "go with flow." Be yourself and allow yourself to be coachable. Don't forget to ask for help when necessary. Other people and opportunities are there for your learning and growing. Realize how important it is to allow this flow. Once we stop learning and growing, once we get too rigid, we succumb to our deathbed and it only becomes a matter of time until we pass on.

WOOD

Picture yourself as if you are a tree. Your trunk is your body, you are rooted in your individuality, your branches are your friends and family, and your leaves are your experiences during this lifetime. A brief lesson in plant biology teaches us how chlorophyll, microscopic components of leaves, utilizes the exposure to sunlight to formulate food through a process called photosynthesis. This is how plants get their nourishment. In actuality, we are fed from our experiences.

Imagine now that these leaves are reflecting upon months of exposure to troubling times, stressful situations and lack of light in your life. Take a lesson from nature. Like the leaves fall in autumn so that new buds can blossom in the spring, so too can you let go of negative experiences and detrimental distractions that block you from feeling joy. Spring will come. You can, once again, thrive. The most important thing I'd like you to take from this discussion is the understanding that your leaves can be transient relationships, exposure to incidents, and touch-and-go moments of awareness. These are processes that take place daily and that foster life. Let go of things or situations that are out of your control.

Consider the four seasons as a metaphor to help you learn how change is the essence of life. All of our relationships, adventures and sensual affairs are processed cognitively and emotionally on a daily basis. Make the conscious choice to let go of anger, fear, resentment, hate, jealousy and desire for revenge. These negative emotions will only prevent you from blossoming into the kind-hearted, compassionate, healthy, hopeful and attractive human being you were designed to be.

THE FIVE ELEMENTS: INTERACTIONS

According to the five elements theory of Traditional Chinese Medicine, qi flows through the body/mind in theoretical "elements" that correspond to particular aspects of human life. Keep in mind that emotions are vibrations, or qi, with particular frequencies that flow through the body. Take a moment to review the illustration of the five elements (*see Figure 3*).

Figure 3: Five Elements Interaction

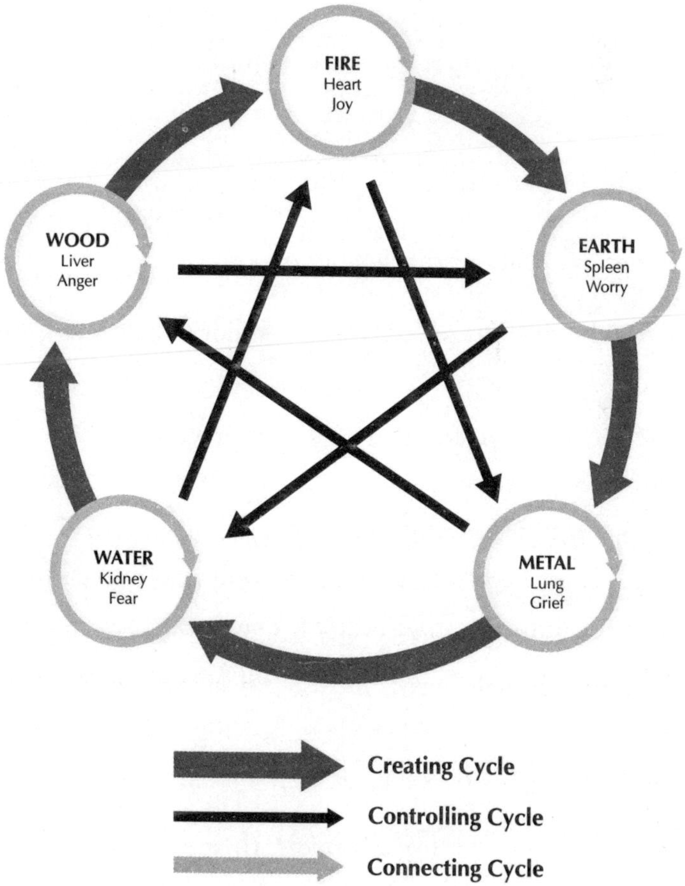

Notice the arrows representing the three ways energy (qi) flows—in a creating, controlling and connecting manner. The concept of the five elements is presented for reasons of personal growth, reconnecting, accepting change and healing. Remember, it's in your nature to heal, just like it's in your nature to be happy and kind.

For example, our water element harbors feelings of fear that affects the flow of energy to the kidneys and bladder. Not only will fear lead to low back pain, but it will hinder your ability to fulfill your passions. As you review the illustration you'll see that water controls fire (where your passions live). Recall, our passionate nature is indicative of the strength of our fire element. So don't let fear drown out your passions in life.

The toxic emotion anger will affect liver function and the flow of energy in the wood element, thereby interfering with the flow of blood through the spleen, as liver qi controls spleen qi. The spleen in Traditional Chinese Medicine assists with blood transformation and body fluid transportation. Hence, if subconsciously blocked, spleen qi becomes stagnant and we can be susceptible to pooling of inflammation, medically diagnosed as edema. Stay rooted in who you are and the happy, loving-kind person you were meant to be.

Follow this last example by noting how energy flows from the Earth element to the water element. We've already learned how the subtle maladaptive stress response to worry or anxiety will perpetuate gastritis, indigestion or reflux disease. If the stress of anxiety gets out of control, it will contribute to the fueling of fears as Earth qi controls the flow of water qi (kidney and bladder).

If you are interested in these concepts and how they relate to our life and our health, they can be better understood by reading Dr. Dianne M. Connelly's book *Traditional Acupuncture: The Law of the Five Elements*.

Chapter Seven

JUXTAPOSING EMOTIONS

Millions of people have become so used to not being happy that
they barely even recognize it.
— Dan Baker, Ph.D.

Are you able to recognize the difference between feeling gratitude and feeling appreciative? There is a subtle difference, and it's one worth pondering. In this intellectual world of ours the distinction will become easier to recognize when we extrapolate the differences on a cognitive level first.

APPRECIATION VERSUS GRATITUDE

Let's look more closely at the intricacies between receiving a gift and claiming an award. Receiving a gift is often something unexpected and leads to a feeling of *appreciation* for an act of kindness or thoughtfulness. On the other hand, receiving an award generates a feeling of *gratitude* because the award was most likely earned. Do you see the difference? In other words, appreciation is happenstance and gratitude is achieved. Gratitude is always a part of your life if you have put effort into the evolution of accomplishment. Living in the mode of gratitude helps you live with purpose.

The feeling of gratitude is mosaic in nature. It is a combination of thank you, contentment and satisfaction all wrapped up into one experience. Remember, cells thrive and healthfully regenerate when exposed to the frequency generated by feelings of gratitude. Our cells and body/mind also thrive when you practice optimism. Being optimistic means looking for things, events and people in your life that bring you happiness and gratitude. Optimism truly invites a healthier mindset.

JOY VERSUS HAPPINESS

Compare the feeling of joy with the feeling of happiness. *Joy* will sometimes send a shiver to your body or bring you to tears. This emotion can be instantaneous or gradual depending on the situation. For example, while watching a love story on television you might find yourself in the actor's shoes as you shed tears of joy, just from watching expressions of love. Conversely, as you contemplate *happiness* from occurrences in a day, week, month or year, the feelings bring a smile to your face. They facilitate tranquility and contentment for what is. That is because something over time is feeding your bliss. "I want *more* of that," you might think as you delve into feelings of happiness. Run with feelings of happiness as long as you can, because recognizing or realizing what feeds your bliss perpetuates happiness, and happiness is a way of life.

I often ask my patients to verbalize serendipity and let the situation support their ability to see the good in everything. Reminding yourself that life has meaning and life can be quite wonderful is a worthy practice. Your perceptions, in other words, how your senses are transmitting information to your brain, build self-awareness and help you better appreciate your world. Hopefully your perceptions promote the flow of instantaneous joy into your living experience.

Here is an example of how to practice realizing how joyful life can be. When one of your favorite songs comes on the radio don't hesitate to turn it up and say aloud, even if you are alone, "Oh! I *love* this song!" It helps to actually hear yourself say it. Another exercise you may consider is while driving home from work one evening pay special attention to the sunset. Say aloud (again, even if you are alone) something along the lines of, "Wow! What a beautiful sunset. This world we live in is quite spectacular." I have seen many gorgeous sunsets in the Florida Keys, but the ones that really move me are when I see the sky painted like a pink and teal tapestry swirling into the distance and fading out into a yellow-orange horizon. Do your best to keep the positive frequency (thoughts) flowing and continue with some healthy self-talk such as, "Life is good!"

BE OPTIMISTIC

Hearing yourself express positive emotion or good feelings enhances optimism. Do you know the story of Bert and John Jacobs? They are the two brothers from Boston who founded the T-shirts and hats company Life is good®. In 1994, their brainstorming resulted in the image of "Jake" and their now-famous slogan "Life is good." Jake is a cartoon-like stick character with a big smile. His expression enhances the meaning of their slogan. On their clothing he is placed in a variety of roles—playing sports, relaxing in a hammock, or just having fun with his dog. He is an image people can identify with and that elicits feelings people want more of in their lives. Once the Jacobs brothers were able to project a simple message of fun and optimism with their products, their company soared to financial success. "Jake" creates the *feeling* of happiness. He sometimes even gets people to laugh and smile just by looking at him.

One of the key things you need to do to build genuine happiness is laugh and smile more often. Allow some silliness and playfulness into your life. As Dr. Deepak Chopra has said to people who become too serious and stressed out, "Be more child-like." In other words, don't forget to play, laugh, giggle and smile. These actions perpetuate joy and feeling good.

Now, let's juxtapose feelings of joy with appreciation and feelings of happiness with gratitude. In both paradigms these emotions become a noticeable human experience after something good or nice happens. These pleasurable human experiences stimulate the flow of energy in the form of emotion that most people allow with ease. You may consider these experiences serendipitous or choose to recognize them as karma, but either way they give you an opportunity to feel good and comment on the goodness of a situation at hand.

When we take a closer look at the concept of happiness and contemplate the feeling of gratitude, we become aware of the continuum of what is. Happiness and gratitude are always there to be recognized if you give these feelings a chance to inhabit your being. Distractions occur when the ego takes over and when dogmatism and judgmental attitudes prevail. Problems and red flags tend to arise when we take life too seriously. Predicaments caused by solemnity can pull you down into the depths of blame, frustration, and eventually depression. Find the power to change. Make it a point today to think about people, situations and events that bring you perpetual happiness. Repeat the mantra "infinite love & gratitude" as you realize that life is good!

THE POWER TO CHANGE

Cells want to regenerate in a healthy fashion. They want to be rejuvenated and replicate unadulterated. This process will occur naturally and more easily when your body is supported by an optimistic mind. Cells don't choose to be degenerative, dysplastic or cancerous. It's very important to know that our cells have the capacity to regenerate healthy tissues whether they are five years old, forty-five years old or eighty years old.

It has been said that "age" is a state of mind. The truth in this statement reveals to us an ancient wisdom. That wisdom is the power to change the way we are thinking, especially when it comes to overcoming health challenges. If you keep telling yourself you are getting old and decrepit, you are sure to accelerate the degenerative process we see in geriatric patients and you are sure to experience aches, pains and arthritis. Remember, one of the rules to mastering this game of life is respecting, honoring and accepting that you will experience pain, fear and challenges. That doesn't mean you have to succumb to them. It just means you have an opportunity to learn more about yourself, be creative and overcome the challenges; an opportunity to rise to the occasion!

If you can fully appreciate the fact that you are getting wiser, becoming more aware, making healthier choices in your food plan and exercise program, and practicing meditation, then you will continue to thrive well into your nineties. Miracles occur every day. Let yourself experience one today.

Be aware of goodness in all situations. See the world like a young child and allow space for the feeling of amazement. Respect that feeling, appreciate it and comment on it. Talk to yourself every single day. Give yourself positive affirmations on how good you are feeling.

Here's an invaluable tip for you to practice that will foster belief in yourself and enhance your ability to overcome challenges. Look into your eyes in the mirror each morning when you brush your teeth and say to yourself, "You are awesome...have a great day!" You may laugh and think it's silly, but incantations like this one instill a steadfast confidence and faith in who you are and what you are. They also give you the power to change when you are feeling lost or stuck.

KNOWING YOUR EMOTIONS

Feeling nervous often arises in situations such as when making an important financial decision, giving a public talk, delivering a business presentation, or performing a musical solo. Nervousness may hit you as you are about to meet the woman or man of your dreams. The feeling of nervousness is sometimes confused with the feeling of excitement. Both feelings will elevate your blood pressure and increase your pulse rate. Both can stimulate a cold sweat or cause dry mouth.

If you focus on the feeling of being nervous, you risk letting that distract your ability to pull off a great performance. If you can allow and appreciate that the feeling is more excitement than nervousness, you can open the door to a great show. As a result, you can then give yourself credit for rising to the occasion and, in turn, look forward to future opportunities to perform and share your talents again. If you give too much credence to the nervousness or apparent anxiety, you may choose to forego the ensuing invitation, whether it is to speak again or jam with some awesome musicians. So let go of interpreting the feeling as nervousness, anxiety or worry. Instead, envision yourself performing onstage and receiving a standing ovation. Aspire to blow 'em away with a whirlwind musical solo.

During a trip to Israel, my friend Dr. Clifford Shooker was warmly greeted by a cousin who was throwing a party in his honor. As director of a performing arts theatre, Cliff's cousin Roy had professional musicians as friends. Knowing Cliff's avocation as a musician, Roy invited several musicians to play at the party. Roy introduced the performers to the party guests. To Cliff's surprise, rather than jamming together, Roy had arranged for Cliff to follow the other musicians with a performance of his own. He was to follow highly respected, internationally known musicians.

As the first performance got underway, Cliff was torn between enjoying the acoustic beauty of a brilliant pianist accompanied by a soprano vocalist and the sickening reaction of a gurgling stomach when he realized he was out of his league. He was sure of the latter after a dazzling Brazilian guitar-flute duet.

When it came time for Cliff to blow his rented saxophone, he explained to the audience that he was an intermediate player and didn't deserve to share the stage with such accomplished musicians. Even his inner thighs were sweating as he expressed his respect for the others who performed before him.

As Cliff got up to play he asked if someone would accompany him. The jazz guitarist volunteered. Absent having anything prepared, Cliff asked for a blues progression, which the guitarist happily provided.

The American tenderfoot took a couple of deep breaths and blew his horn with a divine guidance, never missing a single note. In fact he played as well as he had ever played! He told me it was the feeling of respect and humility that allowed him to perform with such flow and consistency. He simply felt the musical vibration in his soul, released his nervousness, and expressed his verve for life through his music.

Applause erupted and Cliff knew he had pulled off one on the best performances of his life so far as a saxophonist. He had let go of being nervous and fearful. He stood up there and channeled the love and respect he had for the better players. You could say he tapped into their talent pool and chased away his *thinking* that he wasn't good enough. It just *felt* right; it felt good and his fingers cooperated with every breath.

Once again we become aware of the differences between *thinking* and *feeling*. Understanding the importance of taking a moment to unravel and extrapolate exactly what you're feeling or sensing prepares you for greatness—in that awareness of your feelings and in knowing you have a choice, the ultimate guidance becomes available.

JOY HEALS THE HEART

As I've discussed, every organ system in the body has a tendency to attract certain frequencies associated with particular emotions. According to the wisdom of Traditional Chinese Medicine, anger goes to the liver, worry and anxiety to the stomach, sadness and grief to the lungs, fear to the kidneys and bladder, and so on…Well, much to our benefit, joy and appreciation go directly to the heart. Remember Linda in Chapter 1? Our biggest focus was on repairing any damage to her heart with the energy from an abundance of joy. I helped her imagine people, situations and events that created a healing frequency and instantaneously healed her heart.

Be aware though, we cannot hold on to joy by thinking that there is not enough to go around. That scarcity mentality leads to problems that perpetuate symptoms such as constipation and sometimes even congestive heart failure. Trying to hold on to joy is like trying to hold water or trying to hold sand. It somehow keeps leaking out through the cracks between our fingers or overflows with subtle changes of hand position.

Please know that there is plenty of joy to experience in this life. Look for the beauty in this world and recognize it as your truth. If you are thinking you had better hold on to the memory of yesterday's fun and adventure, let it go! Chances are tomorrow holds better and more fulfilling times for you, times capable of feeding your heart with an abundance of joy.

A HEART WALL

There is something called a "heart wall" that can develop in people. It is akin to a callus that forms on your hand after tiring, laborious efforts. It's as if you apparently cannot feel anything due to a protective coat of armor around your heart. The arrow of love headed straight for your heart cannot penetrate the wall, and you lose a prospective companion. Then you spend countless hours and days wondering why there doesn't seem to be quality people available to love and with whom to share your life.

A heart wall can be softened with a conscious effort to forgive and a conscious effort to "feel out" situations. This metaphysical diagnosis is very real when it comes to the challenges of getting back on track to thriving. It is as real as a medical diagnosis of fibromyalgia or syndrome "X" and it is overcome by changing a toxic lifestyle and changing the way you view your world.

Fibromyalgia is, simply put, a fibrous coating laid down upon the muscle tendons that causes pain and is accompanied by insomnia. The way to overcome it is to practice the five basics of maintaining health I mentioned in Chapter 5. Daily exercise, fish oil supplementation, and relaxation/preparatory routines before going to bed are invaluable to overcome fibromyalgia. I have given you some routines throughout this book. You should be taking these steps if you are experiencing this medical diagnosis. You want to move in the right direction to overcoming this experience. Remain hopeful—it *is* possible to heal from fibromyalgia. Acupuncture also will facilitate the healing process.

Syndrome "X" is named for its catalog of symptoms including nervousness, anxiety, headaches, palpitations and insomnia, basically due to insulin resistance and sugar metabolism imbalances. It is now more commonly called Metabolic Syndrome or Met-S and can lead to developing Type II diabetes. If you are experiencing this conglomeration of symptoms, change your food plan by decreasing sugar intake and cutting out processed foods. Drink more pure filtered water. Remove aspartame (Nutra-Sweet) and sucralose (Splenda) from your diet, and begin to love yourself unconditionally. These changes will be a step in the right direction to overcoming this *dis*-ease.

There are so many diseases and syndromes we can become victim to if we succumb to them. The first and foremost thought you should have during these times of *dis*-ease is, "I want to feel better!" or, "I want to feel good!" This should be your first goal every single day. That way, when you are moving into thoughts and situations that make you feel good, you are going to create or manifest more feel-good moments, leaving no chance of developing a heart wall.

THOUGHTS ARE THINGS

If you can bring yourself to believe that thoughts are things, then you can have anything you want. We can have anything we want when we put our minds to it, so you can transform bad feelings into good feelings, right?

The brilliant personal-success author Napoleon Hill once said, "You become what you think about, most of the time." Or more appropriately put, you *get* what you think about most of the time. This is the Law of Attraction, a supreme law that is foundational to other laws scientists have validated such as the law of gravity or the law of thermodynamics. These are examples of laws that pertain to living here on Earth.

The law of gravity reveals to us, quite realistically, that if we were to step off a roof we would certainly fall to the ground and probably hurt ourselves. But the law of gravity has a supreme law that is apparently nullified by what is called the law of lift. The law of lift shows us that when we can accelerate at a high enough speed and with the proper wing span, we can be lifted and fly without falling to the ground no matter if we are 200 pounds, 2000 pounds or even a 900,000-pound 747 jet!

These supreme laws are ones that we must be aware of so we can better choose our actions and more easily make a shift when challenging times become overwhelming. Let's consider the most supreme and undeniable law, the Law of Attraction. You've probably read or heard of the book *The Secret* or seen the film, and may have heard of the Abraham-Hicks teachings, but perhaps you are still wondering how and why it all works. It is not up to us to ask how or why our universe is the way it is. That will only stress us out. Everything is the way it should be! If you don't like it, start making changes today. It all starts with thinking and tapping into what is called a pure potentiality.

So, what do you think about each and every day? Are you thinking, "Oh woe is me?" Or are you thinking, "Wow, this is a perfect opportunity to prove to myself that I can overcome anything?" Imagine thinking this: "I have certainly been under a lot of stress lately, and I seem to be feeling under the weather, but I know I can turn this thing around. It all starts with my thoughts." If you can think like this, you are on the right track! Thoughts are measurable frequencies that begin the manifesting process.

DEVELOPING WISDOM

The energy of thought or cognition sometimes never gets to travel to the heart. In other words, thoughts are not always on the forefront of feelings. At times we do not take advantage of or even access our built-in guidance system. This is called living in a state of anoesis, or passive consciousness without understanding—it is a state in which there is not a conscious connection between our thoughts and our feelings. The approximately thirteen inches between the brain and the heart become a road less traveled due to disconnecting, denying and/or defending, thereby hindering the developing of wisdom.

I make sure my patients understand that these types of patterns are not weaknesses, but examples of how we protect ourselves. These patterns arise and are affected by subconscious patterns of survival that have developed not to protect our brains, lungs, liver or kidneys, but to protect our spirits.

Another form of protection we back into is the "fright, flight or fight" mode. This is better known in Western medicine as the hypothalamic/pituitary/adrenal axis. An example of this mode is depicted by the story we've all heard of the 105–pound mom who is able to lift a car as her baby is trapped beneath it. This example reveals the power of the mind and how it amplifies infinite possibilities and human potential. This is just another example of how miracles can occur.

When we are aware of our thoughts and emotions we are better equipped to use the tools, strategies and support systems available to us to overcome challenges. As long as we can remain honest with our emotions and creative with our options, we can thrive. If we practice completing life experiences we will develop wisdom and enjoy an honorable existence. This not only helps us establish emotional stability but sets the table for acts of compassion. Remember, compassion is the force that holds this universe together. You have an opportunity to do your part. If we have too many incomplete life experiences we will become helpless, hopeless and tightrope-walk the verge to giving up!

What do you choose? That's what I thought…You choose *LOVE*. So get to work! Think, breathe, feel and act out of kindness. Recognize that by practicing this sequence you are developing wisdom and creating easy access to the happiness within you.

Chapter Eight

LIFE IS GOOD

The journey of a thousand miles begins with a single step.
— Lao Tzu

A discipline of mine is to meditate daily. As I've discussed earlier, there are many benefits to be derived from this practice. Meditation helps me achieve equanimity, which means peace of mind. I've loved the word equanimity since I first encountered it. In 2002 I was beginning my studies in Asian philosophy and the teachings of Buddha and I was immensely attracted to the meaning of equanimity and the potential it suggested—it fit with my views on life and how I wanted to live it. I'm not sure what drew me to the study of Asian philosophy and Buddhism at that time, which was a transitional time in my life, but I am grateful for the synchronicity and I trust that everything happens for a reason.

Taoism, Buddhism and Zen Buddhism are all philosophies that ring true for me, and they have since I was a kid growing up in eastern Massachusetts. I didn't have much exposure to these philosophical practices when I was young, but the fundamental ideas have always attracted me—I didn't know what those practices entailed, nor was I in an environment that believed in them or taught them. Parochial school, nuns and Catholicism were all I knew when it came to religion and spirituality. There are subtle differences between these practices that I am not going to elaborate on here—instead, I am going to discuss how I began to learn about and incorporate these philosophies into my life. There are many wonderful books you can consult to deepen your knowledge—and perhaps in a future book, I will elaborate on the distinctions between these practices myself! But for now, I'll describe the beginning of my path to you.

I was first attracted to the book *Awakening the Buddha Within* by Lama Surya Das in early 2002. This is a book on Tibetan wisdom and it teaches eight steps to enlightenment. I was, at the time, just beginning to accept the practice of kinesiology and understand muscle reflex testing as a tool to incorporate into my chiropractic practice. To me, kinesiology was a great gift. At first it was a mystery—it seemed an eso-teric way of addressing the human body to facilitate healing. I wasn't sure how muscle testing worked. Similarly, I was not familiar with the profundity of the Tao or Buddhism, but I just devoured all of this new knowledge like a hungry dog. With the Tao, I felt like I found a long lost love—one that fit me and my belief system like an old pair of faded jeans.

Since studying the Tao, I realized that its fundamental ideas have always correlated with my views on life. In other words, the Tao was something I believed in although I never even knew who Lao Tzu was. As I began my studies, I learned that he was a man who lived about twenty-five hundred years ago and who wrote and taught the eighty-one passages that make up the Tao—a Chinese word meaning "the way." I think everyone should read the Tao and honor it as truth. If you haven't read the *Tao Te Ching* by Lao Tzu, make it a point to do so very soon. You can choose to read Dr. Wayne Dyer's interpretation of Lao Tzu's work in his book *Change Your Thoughts, Change Your Life*, or an actual translation. There are several good versions of the translation. Read a passage every morning and contemplate the necessary changes you need to make to follow its undeniably important messages. It will change your life for the better!

A DAILY PRACTICE

I start my day with a routine and then stay as flexible as possible to bring balance to the next fifteen or so hours, which will surely entail work and play. When we can say, with enthusiasm, "Life is good!" then we have most likely lived a day filled with a healthy portion of fun along with work, rest, play and solitude. After my morning meditation, I choose to satiate myself on *many* levels. This means creating pleasure for all six senses, which helps support the fact that I'm alive and well! The six senses are:

1. Seeing

2. Smelling

3. Hearing

4. Tasting

5. Touching

6. Feeling/Intuiting

If you don't have one already, create a healthy morning discipline for yourself soon. It gives you a whole new outlook on the day.

Morning meditation, as I mentioned, is step one! Basically, we meditate to be happy and to create the awareness that happiness *is* in our life. Here are three steps to follow:

1. Be present; bring your attention to the "now"

2. Dive into the mode of appreciation; create a gratitude list

3. Bathe in the vibrations of love; love will surely titillate all six of your senses

After thirty minutes of primordial sound meditation, which I learned at The Chopra Center, I begin filling my senses with some of the finer things in life. For me, at this time every morning, I truly enjoy a hot cup of bold, black coffee.

Every day I sit on my front porch and look out over the bay, paying close attention to birds, butterflies, bees, flowers and trees. I can't help but notice the sun's rays emerging as sparkles dancing across the water. I sip hot, black, roasted coffee, which according to some people, is not healthy. But to me…it is *quite* healthy. The coffee contributes to my overall feeling of appreciation, to a morning ritual in which I choose to indulge. In terms of my senses, I tantalize the aromatic receptors of my brain with a roasted coffee bouquet and titillate my taste buds by drinking a cup or two of the jubilant java. The magical bean extract ventures to my brain in the form of caffeine as I willingly indulge in one of the finer things in life. This early morning time is in some ways an extension of my meditation. It complements and adds to the vibrations of gratitude.

Did you know that one of the healthiest things you can do for yourself is to rest your mind? As you've learned, you rest your mind by increasing the gap between thoughts. That means if you're not already meditating, learn to meditate! With regards to the theme of your meditation, you can choose to attract a world of possibilities involving fun and adventure, or you can choose to imagine a new business you are planning to start. You can choose to work on manifesting your reality, or focus on, for example, the profound concept of emptiness. Either way, meditation is healthy for you. Meditative thoughts create electrical waves that emit from your brain. What you think about most of the time, becomes your reality, so be conscious of what you are doing and why you are doing it.

Think of things that bring you pleasure. I am not advising you start your day with a chocolate truffle and a shot of Kahlua in your coffee. The thought alone is decadent. The point is that the mind doesn't know the difference between imagination and reality, so bodily responses are more likely to be pleasant if the thoughts are pleasant.

Being conscious of your thoughts and understanding that they create your reality is critically important. Ever wonder why something seemingly random and inexplicable pops up in your life? For instance, why would a person who is very positive and seemingly happy experience a car accident? One possible explanation has to do with the attractor field you are creating with your thoughts. For a few moments while driving, you might dwell on a challenging situation. The next thing you know, feelings of frustration or fear arise. The energy associated with the frustration or fear becomes a wavelength that travels around your ambient field of energy. That ambient field of energy is now a magnetic-like force. Believe it or not, someone else is thinking about something that's frustrating or scary, and boom! Collision! That's how the attractive forces of frustration and/or fear may create an auto accident. Conversely, things on your mind that emit joy and appreciation may attract a more positive experience into your life. Instead of saying, "Be *careful* what you wish for," I suggest, "Be *conscious* of what you wish for."

Remember, thoughts are things that can actually be measured. They create a biochemical reaction in the body. Serotonin is a chemical neurotransmitter secreted in the brain that stimulates mood. Painful thoughts, for example, witnessing an accident on the highway leads people to feeling bad, even though they are not involved in the accident. On the other hand, pleasurable thoughts, and acts of kindness gently stimulate the brain to increase serotonin levels, which pave your way to feeling happy or good. Did you know that your serotonin level rises just by witnessing an act of kindness? Not only do the people giving kindness and the people receiving kindness benefit by increased serotonin levels, but also the people watching the act have a biochemical burst of feeling good!

The joys I derive from my morning routine shape my life and empower my choice to thrive. The thoughts I somehow tap into are not physical, but magical. I indulge and float in a cloud of appreciation nearly every morning. It's like snuggling up to a warm fire or getting a chill as you wrap yourself in a fluffy, down-feather comforter.

When you are looking for the answers to life's toughest questions, such as, "Who am I?" and, "How can I accept that everything is as it should be?" If you are not balanced and maintaining a sense of equilibrium and a positive flow of thoughts, your decisions will be affected, most likely, by a *troubled* mind. This state indicates that you've succumbed to the sentiment that life is not easy. But as I have mentioned before, life doesn't present us with anything that we can't handle. We must be open to finding the tools, strategies and support we need to overcome challenges and stay peaceful.

THERE ARE NO COINCIDENCES

Everything in life happens for a reason. In this book, I hope I inspired you to stay positive as you learned the principles of building genuine happiness and living in appreciative joy. Make these principles your own and put them into practice. I hope I inspired you for further growth so you will have easy access to the feeling of peace within you. You can stay positive much easier and longer when you tap into the awareness that *everything is love* expressing itself the best way it can under the circumstances. This means that even anger is love expressing itself in a different form under that specific situation, perhaps proving that you still care.

We need to be more aware of how we can transform trying situations into opportunities to learn and grow. We learn and grow by recognizing our mistakes. After all, you know yourself better than anyone else does. So take on the attitude of being creative when challenges arise as opposed to being helpless and/or hopeless.

LIFE IS EASY

Life is easy when you study the teachings of the *Tao*, practice patience and forgiveness, and always look for the good in everything. Stay positive by being optimistic. We can tell when we are focusing on the negative, when we blame, judge and criticize, and when we find ourselves complaining about what is wrong. Start developing tools, strategies and support systems for overcoming your challenges. It may be difficult at first, but you need to make it a priority for your and your family's well-being. By practicing this attitude time after time, staying positive and happy will become your second nature.

Remember Rumi, the great Sufi poet and his words of wisdom: "Out beyond ideas of wrongdoing and rightdoing, there is a field. I will meet you there." Think about it. Each time you read this quote and make it your own you will be a step closer to developing genuine happiness, and life will become easier for you.

EVERYTHING IS WORKING PERFECTLY

Imagine a time lapse sequence of the grass growing in your front yard. Doesn't it shoot up out of the ground with ease and enthusiasm for life, an excitement to grow and a desire to feel the warmth of the sun? This is life showing you how easy things can be when you simply welcome each day with moments of peace and acceptance for what is.

Picture this. You have just purchased a new home and you begin to spruce up the grounds by jumping into a landscaping project. The front loader, backhoe and bulldozer have left you a few hundred feet of landfill and rocks. Trees are damaged by the recent construction and the only color outside your new home is dirt-laden gray. Are you angry at the construction workers?

You are not angry at the construction workers for what appears to be a mangled-up front yard; you are simply not happy with its present-time appearance. You are not frustrated by the lack of color embellishing your new home; you are just overwhelmed with change and not accepting the way things are at that moment.

Frustrated with the task ahead? Feeling broke? Be aware of what's going on in your mind as you are looking to express landscape creativity to adorn your new property. These challenges certainly can activate what is known as a "monkey mind." But now you have this book as a reference to help you maintain emotional stability. And deep down inside, you know your life can be easier. As a matter of fact, life moves forward effortlessly when you just go with the flow, right? So...are you angry or not happy? Frustrated or not accepting? This is your opportunity to transform your views of your world and look forward to a new day.

As I've discussed earlier, it is much easier to recognize and move toward the polar opposite of a negative emotion than it is to jump straight to a lot of pleasurable feelings. So, move towards those feelings in steps by creating an action that supports the transition. Start creating good karma for yourself by taking positive action!

Realize that when you are angry, you are actually feeling *not joyful*. That's a different way of looking at it, don't you think? Otherwise you are victim to a subconscious pattern of the toxic emotion of anger. Your continued resistance to changing your emotional state creates mind chatter that leads you astray and affects your judgment. You may feel the urge to blame. That is a normal human tendency. But realize you must change the way you are looking at things and use your support system to adjust your habitual tendency.

As you work to make these changes, communicate what you are working on with someone you love and who loves you. In this way, you not only enlist support, but learn and grow from the interaction and the challenges you are tackling. Our means of communication with others, as well as with ourselves through self-talk, create either positive or negative results. Make the choice to create positivity. Be more aware of your thinking. Be kind to yourself. Surrounding yourself with positivity will be a key to effectively and efficiently overcoming stress and will help you focus your mind so it becomes a *trained* monkey! Remember everything is as it should be and as my friend Mari-Etta Stoner believes, "Everything is working perfectly!"

PEACEFUL EASY FEELINGS

A well-respected, wise and learned Hindu sage was asked, "What is it like to be in Satori?" He responded, "It is living here on earth, here and now, only two inches above the ground." Whether you call it Satori, Nirvana, Utopia, or heaven on earth, it sounds good, right? But can we achieve that state? Yes, we all can! One way to get there is to let go of the heavy feelings of anxiety, worry, anger, blame, and most importantly, refrain from letting your ego run your life. Experiencing these states of mind and wonderful feelings can occur in daily life right here on this beautiful, breathing, nurturing planet.

Have you ever experienced the sensation of floating? It comes around when you are feeling in love. Remember? It's when you are so enmeshed in happiness and togetherness that everything seems to go your way. The more you allow this feeling and the more you allow people into your life, the more you can perpetuate the feelings of bliss. Your life is about sharing and serving and in those character-filled actions we find the shift to feeling consistently happy and at peace. The take-away is simply this: Peaceful, easy feelings are cultivated and nurtured when we practice meditation, random acts of kindness, and boundless compassion.

APPENDIX

THE LIFELINE TECHNIQUE®

The LifeLine Technique® is one of the primary tools I use in evaluating and treating patients. It is an extremely effective system that has transformed my approach to healing and has helped thousands of my patients. I refer to The LifeLine Technique several times throughout *The Wisdom of Emotions*, especially when presenting the healing experiences of my patients. As I mention in the text, the advice contained in these pages is not dependent on The LifeLine Technique—while it is a valued tool, cultivating happiness is available to anyone, anywhere. For those interested in learning more, here is background information on the technique.

Developed by my longtime friend and valued colleague, Dr. Darren Weissman, the LifeLine Technique is both an ancient and advanced complete system of transformation and wholeness. The LifeLine Technique is a philosophy, science and quantum technology that bridges gaps between the conscious and subconscious mind. At the root of every symptom, stress and disease is a subconscious emotional pattern of reaction. When activated this pattern of reaction will cause both behavioral and biological stressors. The cornerstone of The LifeLine Technique is our view of symptoms, stress and disease. Rather than something being wrong with a person, symptoms, stress and disease are the language your body and life use to awaken you to your authentic power of transformation and create change. The LifeLine Technique enables you to activate your subconscious mind and thus have a direct impact on genetic expressions affecting the health of your body and the relationships in your life.

We focus on the Five Basics for Optimal Health—the quantity, quality and frequency of water, food, rest, exercise and owning your power.

Anyone can be trained to be a Certified LifeLine Practitioner as long as you are passionate about taking responsibility for your life and consciously bringing out your best. There are currently Certified LifeLine Practitioners throughout the world.

For more information, please visit:

www.DrDarrenWeissman.com

ACKNOWLEDGMENTS

Many people have provided inspiration and encouragement for this book to become a reality. First and foremost I want to express my deepest gratitude to my wife Susan. Without her love for me and support for what I do, and without her welcoming the growth of our relationship in this life, I would never have written this book. Her love and her unwavering belief in me are an incredible gift. Thank you Susan, I know now we have shared unconditional love for many lifetimes!

To my parents, Elaine and Dr. Frank Coppola, thank you for always supporting me and fulfilling my needs and desires. Mom, thank you for your unconditional love. It has empowered me and kept me feeling special and important. Dad, you truly have been an example of success, not to mention quite a

tough act to follow. Because of you and your actions both inside and outside of your practice, I have learned how to provide
sound judgment and excellence in health care to my patients as
you do to yours.

I would like to thank my beautiful children, Marissa and
Daniel, for being in my life. Thank you, kids, for choosing me
to be your dad. You continue to bring me joy, make me proud,
and teach me invaluable lessons that I hope to incorporate into
a future book on the *Wisdom of Children*.

To my four sisters, Dianne, Darlene, Deborah, and Donna,
and their families, this book is a result of many experiences
and lessons I've learned, beginning in childhood. You all are so
valued in my life and I greatly respect your individuality. Thank
you for laughing at my jokes and listening to my profound
views on life. And thank you for taking such great care of me
through the years and making me—your *only* brother—feel
like King David!

I would like to thank my mother-in-law, Huang Xirong, and
my bother-in-law, Zhou Shi'an, along with his wife, Yu Ting,
for their unfailing generosity and considerate manner. Family
is truly something to cherish. In every trip I've made to China
to visit them they have treated me with unconditional care and
shown great concern for my well-being. Their approach to life
is proof that appreciating the simple things in life fosters inner
peace and contentment.

ACKNOWLEDGMENTS

I am grateful for the serendipitous relationship with my editor, Andrea Gollin. She is so brilliant and excellent at what she does. I sincerely thank you, Andrea, for going above and beyond. You took the time to really grasp what I teach and edit with such synergy. Your guidance throughout the whole process of writing and publishing has been invaluable.

Dr. Darren Weissman, you are my dear friend, inspiration and mentor in many ways. I often think of our connection and continue to cherish the best of times. Traveling with you in Asia, attending your LifeLine seminars, and enjoying the finer things in life together have greatly contributed to the wisdom I've developed. Your presence in my life, once again, is a blessing.

Dr. Clifford Shooker, thank you for your friendship, the story of you jamming in Israel, and the time you took to read my manuscript. I am always amazed by your intelligence and by the way you see the world. Your insight, generosity and sincerity affirm to me that our first meeting, on a street corner fourteen years ago, was meant to be.

Frank Hawkins, you are an admirable person who combines acuity with creativity, kindness with integrity. Sometimes in life we befriend people with such outstanding character and wisdom, it is difficult to put gratitude into words. Thank you for reading my manuscript and for your advice. As an entrepreneur, businessman and author yourself, you will always be a measure of success to me and to Susan.

Wo de lao wai (in Chinese: my foreign buddy), Victor Sun and Liu Jinbo were instrumental in producing the videos and photographs for this book. Victor, thank you for introducing me to your friends in China and contributing your time and artistic talents. Your publishing savvy was invaluable.

Video Dave Kay, you are so generous and fun to be with. You've been that way since we went to *different* high schools *together*. Thank you for providing the beautiful sunrise photos for the book's cover. Remember, "If you need anything, I'll call you!"

I would like to thank my colleagues with whom I share offices in South Florida. I hold in high regard my associates, doctors Lissa Nirenberg and Susana May. You both are always interested in discussing effective and efficient ways to help people. Irene Nichols, you are one of the best at teaching the Laws of Attraction. Your enthusiasm as a life coach and spiritual counselor are commendable. I will never forget the opportunity my dear friend Dr. Sara Badano gave me. Sharing an office together at Mariners Hospital was a breakthrough for our community. It helped people recognize and appreciate the benefits of fusing Eastern and Western medicine. Sara, you are truly one of the most compassionate and effective medical doctors I have ever had the pleasure to know! Your warm, caring manner and humility are exemplary.

To the Certified LifeLine Practitioners around the world, you are the best of the best! I am honored to be your colleague. And as Darren says, keep shining! To my three best friends from graduate school, doctors Adam Henby, Salim Bohsali, and Kris Gongaware, I will always cherish our friendship and value our brotherhood.

There are people in my life who nourish my existence and whom I recognize as blessing in many ways. Brooke Spaulding and Robert Guzina, thank you both for stimulating my intellectual growth and supporting my emotional well-being. Our conversations are so much fun and always seem to crescendo into joy and appreciation for what is. Ewa and Peter Schwarz, you guys are unbelievable in perpetuating the pursuit of happiness. Thank you for reminding me how to truly appreciate life.

To my long time friends Ed Hughes, Gary Johnson, and college buddy Steve Casagrande, I truly cherish the bonds we've developed since growing up and our continued camaraderie over the past several decades. My south Florida compadres Nick Bangos, Philippe Douillet, and Kent Post, thank you for your support during an intense transitional period in my life. I continue to appreciate our friendships. Cary Walker, thank you for sharing your incredible intelligence and fun-loving attitude with me. And to a person who has been steadfast in her belief in me and encouraged me to start a practice in the fabulous Florida Keys, Jackie Weitzel, thank you for your endless love and support.

Thank you to the inspirational leaders, authors and teachers from whom I have learned and who have helped me become the doctor I am today. I extend my deepest appreciation to doctors Deepak Chopra, David Simon, Vasant Lad, Fu Di, James Winterstein, David Hawkins, Brian Weiss, Bruce Lipton and Wayne Dyer.

To Gregg Braden, Caroline Myss and Louise Hay, I will do my best to tell the world of your invaluable work, research and findings, through which you help humanity realize the fact that we are all capable of healing ourselves from any condition or *dis*-ease. It all starts with education and belief. Thank you, thank you, thank you.

Finally, to the Keys To Peace organization in the fabulous Florida Keys, and in particular, Denise Downing, Ron Cole, Marilyn Rogers, Mari-Etta Stoner, Cheryll Woolf, Dianne Terrasi and Mimi Greek, your presence in this world makes it a better place. All of you are examples of peace, love and happiness. I have learned something from all of you and I am grateful to be considered your friend and colleague. You're right Mari-Etta, everything *is* working perfectly. In joy, we are *all* the Keys To Peace!

RECOMMENDED READING

Awakening the Buddha Within: Tibetan Wisdom for the Western World by Lama Surya Das

The Biology of Belief: Unleashing the Power of Consciousness, Matter, & Miracles by Bruce H. Lipton, Ph.D.

Change Your Thoughts, Change Your Life: Living the Wisdom of the Tao by Dr. Wayne W. Dyer

Comfortable with Uncertainty: 108 Teachings on Cultivating Fearlessness and Compassion by Pema Chodron

Defy Gravity: Healing Beyond the Bounds of Reason by Caroline Myss

The Divine Matrix: Bridging Time, Space, Miracles, and Belief by Gregg Braden

The Eye of the I, From Which Nothing is Hidden by David R. Hawkins, M.D., Ph.D.

The Field: The Quest for the Secret Force of the Universe by Lynne McTaggart

Happiness: Essential Mindfulness Practices by Thich Nhat Hanh

The Heart's Code: Tapping the Wisdom and Power of Our Heart Energy by Paul Pearsall, Ph.D.

Inspiration: Your Ultimate Calling by Dr. Wayne W. Dyer

Molecules of Emotion: The Science Behind Mind-Body Medicine by Candace B. Pert, Ph.D.

The Power of Infinite Love & Gratitude: An Evolutionary Journey to Awakening Your Spirit by Dr. Darren R. Weissman

The Power of Now: A Guide to Spiritual Enlightenment by Eckhart Tolle

The Power Is Within You by Louise L. Hay

The Seven Spiritual Laws of Yoga: A Practical Guide to Healing Body, Mind, and Spirit by Deepak Chopra, M.D. & David Simon, M.D.

RECOMMENDED READING

Traditional Acupuncture: The Law of the Five Elements by Dianne M. Connelly, Ph.D.

What Happy People Know: How the New Science of Happiness Can Change Your Life for the Better by Dan Baker, Ph.D. and Cameron Stauth

ABOUT THE AUTHOR

Dr. David F. Coppola has practiced holistic medicine for over eighteen years. He founded Gables Optimal Health in Coral Gables, FL in 1997, and opened an integrative health care center in the Upper Florida Keys in 1999. He has helped thousands of patients restore health and maintain wellness through every stage of their lives.

Dr. Coppola earned his Bachelor of Science degree in Human Biology from Villanova University and his Doctor of Chiropractic Medicine degree from the National College of Chiropractic. His post-graduate studies include acupuncture at the University of Miami School of Medicine, Total Body Modification (TBM), and certification in The LifeLine Technique®. He has received additional intensive holistic training in Traditional Chinese Medicine, Psychological Traumas Healing, Hormonal Balancing, Ayurveda, Color and Chakra Therapy, and many other forms of energy medicine.

He practices Chiropractic Manipulation, Acupuncture, Massage Therapy and The LifeLine Technique. He is also a life coach who enriches and inspires as he teaches awareness and mindfulness to obtain optimal health. He is grateful to share his wisdom in this book to facilitate his readers' emotional and spiritual journeys to inner peace and happiness.

In addition to his life mission of healings and teachings, Dr. Coppola is an avid musician and travels the world to study and appreciate the wisdom of different cultures. He lives a fun and adventurous life in the fabulous Florida Keys with his wife, Susan, and two children, Marissa and Daniel.

For more information, please visit:

www.DrDavidCoppola.com.

NOTES

NOTES

NOTES

NOTES

NOTES

NOTES

NOTES

NOTES

CHOOSE LOVE
PRESS

QUICK ORDER FORM

- **Online orders: www.DrDavidCoppola.com**
- **Fax orders:** +1 305-567-1974. Send this form.
- **Telephone orders:** Call +1 305-451-1819. Have your credit card ready.
- **Postal Orders:** Choose Love Press
  195 Giralda Avenue
  Coral Gables, FL 33134 USA

Name:_____

Address: _____

City: _____

State/Province: _____ Postal Code: _____

Phone: _____

Email: _____

Payment (Circle payment type): Check or Credit card

Visa   MasterCard   AMEX   Discover

Card number:_____

Name on card: _____

Exp. date: (mm/yy): _____

Please send (   ) copies of **The Wisdom of Emotions**,
USA $20.00 per hardcover book

Shipping and Handling: U.S.: $5.00 for first book,
$2.00 for each additional book

International: Fill out the contact form online at
www.DrDavidCoppola.com

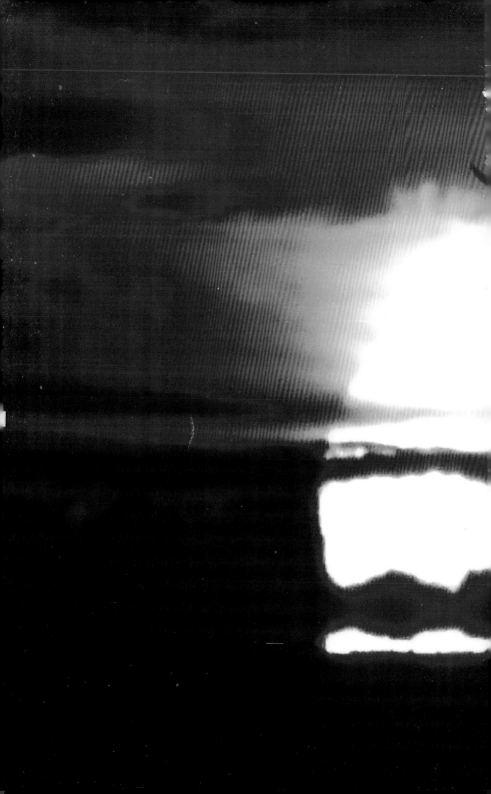